GOVERNMENT PROCEDURES AND OPERATIONS

THE EARNED INCOME TAX CREDIT: OVERVIEW, ECONOMIC ANALYSIS, AND COMPLIANCE CHALLENGES

GOVERNMENT PROCEDURES AND OPERATIONS

Additional books in this series can be found on Nova's website under the Series tab.

Additional e-books in this series can be found on Nova's website under the e-book tab.

GOVERNMENT PROCEDURES AND OPERATIONS

THE EARNED INCOME TAX CREDIT: OVERVIEW, ECONOMIC ANALYSIS, AND COMPLIANCE CHALLENGES

JUDITH L. COLLINS
EDITOR

NOVINKA

New York

Library of Congress Cataloging-in-Publication Data

ISBN: 978-1-63485-632-4

Published by Nova Science Publishers, Inc. † New York

CONTENTS

PREFACE

The Earned Income Tax Credit (EITC) is a refundable tax credit available to eligible workers with relatively low earnings. Because the credit is refundable, an EITC recipient need not owe taxes to receive the benefit. The credit is authorized by Section 32 of the Internal Revenue Code (IRC) and administered as part of the federal income tax system. In 2013, a total of $68.1 billion was claimed by 28.8 million tax filers, making the EITC the largest need-tested anti-poverty cash assistance program. This book provides an overview of the EITC, first discussing eligibility requirements for the credit, followed by how the credit is computed and paid; provides data on the growth of the EITC since it was first enacted in 1975; and includes data on the EITC claimed on 2013 tax returns, examining EITC claims by number of qualifying children, income level, tax filing status, and location of residence. Moreover, this book summarizes findings from the 2014 IRS study detailing the factors that can lead to erroneous claims of the credit, and describes the challenges the IRS may face in their efforts to reduce each type of error. It also examines the role of paid tax preparers on EITC error.

In: The Earned Income Tax Credit
Editor: Judith L. Collins

ISBN: 978-1-63485-632-4

Chapter 1

THE EARNED INCOME TAX CREDIT (EITC): AN OVERVIEW*

Gene Falk and Margot L. Crandall-Hollick

SUMMARY

The Earned Income Tax Credit (EITC) is a refundable tax credit available to eligible workers earning relatively low wages. Because the credit is refundable, an EITC recipient need not owe taxes to receive the benefit. Eligibility for and the amount of the EITC are based on a variety of factors, including residence and taxpayer ID requirements, the presence of qualifying children, age requirements for childless recipients, and the recipient's investment income and earned income. Tax filers with income above certain thresholds—these thresholds are based on marital status and number of qualifying children—are ineligible for the credit.

The EITC varies based on a recipient's earnings. Specifically, the EITC equals a fixed percentage (the "credit rate") of earned income until the credit amount reaches its maximum level. The EITC then remains at its maximum level over a subsequent range of earned income, between the "earned income amount" and the "phase-out amount threshold." Finally, the credit gradually decreases to zero at a fixed rate (the "phase-out rate") for each additional dollar of adjusted gross income (AGI) (or earnings, whichever is greater) above the phase-out amount threshold. The specific

* This is an edited, reformatted and augmented version of a Congressional Research Service publication R43805, prepared for Members and Committees of Congress, dated January 19, 2016.

values of these EITC parameters (e.g., credit rate, earned income amount) vary depending on several factors, including the number of qualifying children a tax filer has and his or her marital status. For the 2015 tax year, the maximum EITC for a tax filer without children is $503 per year. In contrast, the 2015 maximum EITC for a tax filer with one child is $3,359 per year; for two children, $5,548 per year; and for three or more children, $6,242 per year.

Two temporary modifications to the EITC were enacted as part of the American Recovery and Reinvestment Act of 2009 (ARRA; P.L. 111-5), extended by P.L. 111-312 and P.L. 112-240, and made permanent by the Protecting Americans from Tax Hikes (PATH) Act (Division Q of P.L. 114-113). The first modification was a larger credit for families with three or more children, while the second reduced the EITC's marriage penalty.

The EITC is provided to individuals and families once a year, in a lump sum payment after individuals and families file their federal income tax return. The credit may be received in one of three ways: (1) a reduction in federal tax liability; (2) a refund from the Treasury if the tax filer has no income tax liability; or (3) a combination of a reduced federal tax liability and a refund. The amount of the credit a tax filer receives is based on the prior year's income, earnings, and family composition (marital status and number of qualifying children). That is, the EITC paid in 2016 will be based on factors from 2015.

The EITC cannot be counted as income in determining eligibility for or the amount of any federally funded public benefit program. An EITC refund that is saved by a tax filer does not count against the resource limits of any federally funded public benefit program for 12 months after the refund is received.

In 2013, a total of $68.1 billion was claimed by 28.8 million tax filers (19% of all tax filers), making the EITC the largest need-tested anti-poverty cash assistance program. In that year, 97% of all EITC dollars were claimed by families with children. However, there was considerable variation in the share of returns claiming the EITC by state, with a greater share filed in certain southern states compared to other regions of the country.

INTRODUCTION

The Earned Income Tax Credit (EITC) is a refundable tax credit available to eligible workers with relatively low earnings. Because the credit is refundable, an EITC recipient need not owe taxes to receive the benefit. The credit is authorized by Section 32 of the Internal Revenue Code (IRC) and administered as part of the federal income tax system. In 2013, a total of $68.1 billion was claimed by 28.8 million tax filers, making the EITC the largest need-tested anti-poverty cash assistance program.

Under current law, the EITC is calculated based on a recipient's earned income, using one of eight different formulas, which vary depending on several factors, including the number of qualifying children a tax filer has (zero, one, two, or three or more) and his or her marital status (unmarried or married). All else being equal, the amount of the credit tends to increase with the number of eligible children the EITC claimant has. Indeed, most of the benefits of the EITC— 97% of EITC dollars in 2013—go to families with children.

Two temporary modifications to the EITC were enacted under the American Recovery and Reinvestment Act of 2009 (ARRA; P.L. 111-5), extended by P.L. 111-312 and P.L. 112-240, and made permanent by the Protecting Americans from Tax Hikes (PATH) Act (Division Q of P.L. 114-113). The first modification was a larger credit for families with three or more children, while the second reduced the EITC's marriage penalty.

This report provides an overview of the EITC, first discussing eligibility requirements for the credit, followed by how the credit is computed and paid. The report then provides data on the growth of the EITC since it was first enacted in 1975. Finally the report concludes with data on the EITC claimed on 2013 tax returns, examining EITC claims by number of qualifying children, income level, tax filing status, and location of residence.

ELIGIBILITY FOR THE EITC

A tax filer must fulfill the following requirements to claim the EITC:

1. The tax filer must file a federal income tax return.[1]
2. The tax filer must have earned income.
3. The tax filer must meet certain residency and identification requirements.
4. The tax filer's children must meet relationship, residency, and age requirements to be considered qualifying children for the credit.
5. Childless workers who claim the credit must be between ages 25 and 64. (This age requirement *does not apply* to EITC claimants with qualifying children.)
6. The tax filer's investment income must be below a certain amount.

7. The tax filer must not be disallowed the credit due to prior fraud or reckless disregard of the rules when they previously claimed the EITC.

Additionally, a tax filer with income above a certain dollar amount (labelled as "income where credit=0" in *Table 1*) will be ineligible for the credit. Given that this income level is dependent on the number of qualifying children and marital status of the tax filer, this requirement is discussed in greater detail in the section of the report entitled "Calculating the EITC."

Requirements (1) through (7) are discussed in detail below.

Filing a Federal Income Tax Return

To be eligible for the EITC, a person must file a federal income tax return. Those who do not file a federal income tax return cannot receive the EITC.

The EITC can be claimed by taxpayers filing their tax return as married filing jointly, head of household, or single.[2] Tax filers cannot claim the EITC if they use the filing status of married filing separately. If the tax filer has a qualifying child, the tax filer must include the child's name and Social Security number on a separate schedule (Schedule EIC) filed with the federal tax return.[3]

Earned Income

A tax filer must have earned income to claim the EITC. Earned income for the EITC is defined as wages, tips, and other compensation included in gross income. It also includes net self-employment income (self-employment income after deduction of one-half of Social Security payroll taxes paid by a self-employed individual).

In addition, service members may elect to include combat pay in their earnings when calculating the EITC. All income earned by a member of the Armed Forces while in a designated combat zone is considered combat pay and is normally *not included* in taxable income. However, a tax filer may elect to include combat pay as earnings for the purpose of calculating the EITC.[4] Generally, service members will make this election if it results in a larger credit. (Using combat pay to calculate the EITC does not make the combat pay taxable income.)

Certain forms of income are not considered earnings for the purpose of the EITC. These include pension and annuity income, income of nonresident aliens not from a U.S. business, income earned while incarcerated for work in a prison, and TANF benefits paid in exchange for participation in work experience or community service activities.

Finally, tax filers who claim the foreign earned income exclusion (i.e., they file Form 2555 or Form 2555EZ with their federal income tax return) are ineligible to claim the EITC.[5]

Residency and Identification Requirements

Under current law, an EITC recipient must be a resident of the United States, unless the recipient resides in another country because of U.S. military service. To be eligible for the credit, the tax filer must provide valid Social Security numbers (SSNs) for work purposes[6] for themselves, spouses if married filing jointly, and any qualifying children. (U.S. citizenship is not required to be eligible for the credit. SSNs do not indicate U.S. citizenship.) Nonresident aliens—those that do not spend sufficient time in the United States—are generally ineligible for the EITC.[7]

Qualifying Children

An EITC recipient's qualifying child must meet three requirements.[8] First, the child must have a specific *relationship* to the tax filer (son, daughter, step child or foster child,[9] brother, sister, half-brother, half-sister, step brother, step sister, or descendent of such a relative). Second, the child must share a *residence* with the taxpayer for more than half the year in the United States.[10] Third, the child must meet certain *age requirements*; namely, the child must be under the age of 19 (or age 24, if a full-time student) or be permanently and totally disabled.

As a result of these three requirements, a child may be the qualifying child of more than one tax filer in the same household. For example, a child who lives with a single parent, grandparent, and aunt in the same home could be a qualifying child of all three of these individuals. But only one of these individuals can claim the qualifying child for the EITC, and the others cannot. Indeed, it appears that under current law, the other individuals are also ineligible to claim the childless EITC.[11] In the case where the tax filers cannot agree on who claims the child, there are “tiebreaker” rules for who can claim the child for the EITC.[12]

Age Requirements for EITC Recipients with No Qualifying Children

If a tax filer has *no qualifying children*, he or she must be between 25 and 64 years of age to be eligible for the EITC. There is no age requirement for tax filers *with qualifying children.*

Investment Income

A tax filer with investment income over a certain dollar amount is ineligible for the EITC. The statutory limit—$2,200—is adjusted annually for inflation. For 2015, the limit on investment income is $3,400. Investment income is defined as interest income (including tax-exempt interest), dividends, net rent, net capital gains, and net passive income. It also includes royalties that are from sources other than the filer’s ordinary business activities.

Disallowance of the EITC Due to Fraud or Reckless Disregard of Rules

A tax filer is barred from claiming the EITC for a period of 10 years after the IRS makes a final determination to reduce or disallow a tax filer’s EITC because that individual made a fraudulent EITC claim. A tax filer is barred from claiming the EITC for a period of two years after the IRS determines that the individual made an EITC claim “due to reckless and intentional disregard of the rules” of the EITC, but that disregard was not found to be fraud.[13]

CALCULATING THE EITC

The EITC amount is based on formulas that consider earned income, number of qualifying children, marital status, and adjusted gross income

(AGI). In general, the EITC equals a fixed percentage (the “credit rate”) of earned income until the credit reaches it maximum amount. The EITC then remains at its maximum level over a subsequent range of earned income, between the “earned income amount” and the “phase-out amount threshold.” Finally, the credit gradually decreases in value to zero at a fixed rate (the “phase-out rate”) for each additional dollar of earnings or AGI (whichever is greater) above the phase-out amount threshold. The specific values of these EITC parameters (e.g., credit rate, earned income amount, etc.) vary depending on several factors, including the number of qualifying children a tax filer has and his or her marital status, as illustrated in *Table 1*.

Table 1. EITC Tax Parameters by Marital Status

Number of Qualifying Children	0	1	2	3 or more
unmarried tax filers(single and head of household filers)				
credit rate	7.65%	34%	40%	45%
earned income amount	$6,580	$9,880	$13,870	$13,870
maximum credit amount	$503	$3,359	$5,548	$6,242
phase-out amount threshold	$8,240	$18,110	$18,110	$18,110
phase-outrate	7.65%	15.98%	21.06%	21.06%
income wherecredit = 0	$14,820	$39,131	$44,454	$47,747
married tax filers(married filing jointly)				
credit rate	7.65%	34%	40%	45%
earned income amount	$6,580	$9,880	$13,870	$13,870
maximum credit amount	$503	$3,359	$5,548	$6,242
phase-out amount threshold	$13,750	$23,630	$23,630	$23,630
phase-outrate	7.65%	15.98%	21.06%	21.06%
income wherecredit = 0	$20,330	$44,651	$49,974	$53,267

Source: IRS Revenue Procedure 2014-61 and Internal Revenue Code (IRC) Section 32.

As illustrated in *Table 1*, the EITC’s earned income amounts, credit rates, phase-out rates, and maximum credit amounts vary by the number of qualifying children a tax filer has. The EITC ranges from a maximum credit of $503 for a tax filer without a child to $6,242 for a tax filer with three or more qualifying children, as illustrated in *Figure 1*.

The phase-out amount threshold varies by *both* the number of qualifying children a tax filer has and his or her marital status. The phase-out amount threshold for those who are married filing joint returns is $5,520 greater than for unmarried filing statuses with the same number of children. (Tax filers who file as married filing separately are ineligible for the EITC.)

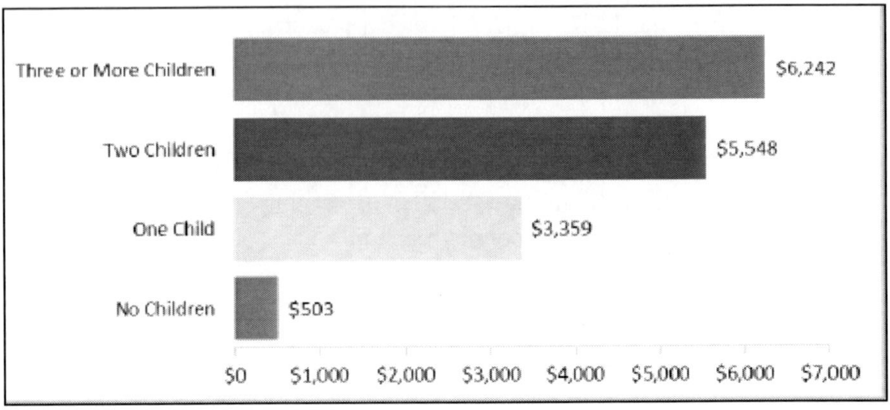

Source: Congressional Research Service based on IRS Revenue Procedure 2014-61 and Internal Revenue Code (IRC) Section 32.

Figure 1. Maximum EITC by Number of Qualifying Children: 2015.

This higher phase-out amount threshold for married tax filers reduces (but generally does not eliminate) potential "marriage penalties" in the EITC whereby the credit for a married couple is less than the combined credit of two unmarried recipients.

Figure 2 illustrates the EITC amount by earnings level for an unmarried taxpayer with one child for 2015. It shows the three distinct ranges of EITC for this family:

- *Phase-in Range:* The EITC increases with earnings from the first dollar of earnings up to earnings of $9,880. Over this earnings range, the credit equals the *credit rate* (34% for a tax filer with one child) times the amount of annual earnings. The $9,880 threshold is called the *earned income amount* and is the earnings level at which the EITC ceases to increase with earned income. The income interval up to the earned income amount, where the EITC increases with earnings, is known as the *phase-in range*.
- *Plateau:* The EITC remains at its maximum level of $3,359 from the earned income amount ($9,880) until earnings exceed $18,1100. The $3,359 credit represents the *maximum credit* for a tax filer with one child in 2015. The income interval with the EITC fixed at its maximum value represents the *plateau* on *Figure 2*.
- *Phase-out Range:* Once earnings exceed $18,110, the EITC is reduced for every additional dollar over that amount. The $18,110 threshold is

known as the *phaseout amount threshold* for a single taxpayer with one child in 2015. For each dollar over the phase-out amount threshold, the EITC is reduced by 15.98%. The 15.98% rate is known as the *phase-out rate*. The income interval from the phaseout income level until the EITC is completely phased out is known as the *phase-out range*.

The EITC is completely phased out (EITC = $0) once the tax filer's AGI (or earned income, whichever is greater) reaches $39,131. The earned income amounts and the phase-out amount thresholds are adjusted each year for inflation.

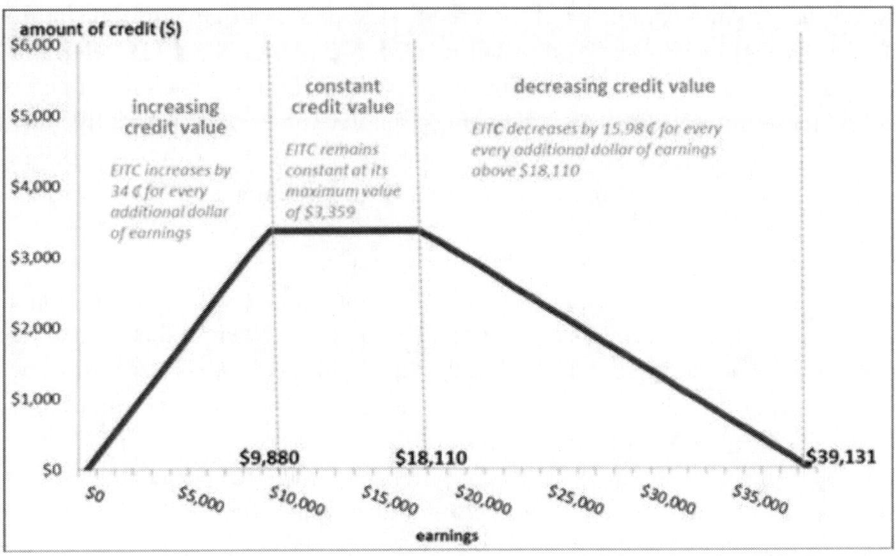

Source: Congressional Research Service, based on information in IRS Revenue Procedure 2014-61 and Internal Revenue Code Section 32.

Figure 2. Amount of the EITC for an Unmarried Tax Filer with One Child, 2015.

In practice, EITC claimants use tables published by the IRS to calculate their credit amount. A tax filer can look up the correct amount of his or her EITC based on income, marital status, and number of qualifying children. The instructions for the federal income tax form[14] show the EITC amounts in tables by income brackets (in $50 increments).

Income Limits for the EITC

As previously discussed, the amount of the EITC is reduced for each dollar of AGI (or earnings, if greater) above a certain dollar threshold, referred to as the phase-out amount threshold. That threshold, combined with the phase-out rate, results in a specific income level (referred to as "income where credit=0" in *Table 1*) above which a tax filer is ineligible for the credit. This income level, where the credit reaches zero, is sometimes referred to as the *eligibility threshold.*

As illustrated in *Table 1*, there are eight eligibility thresholds for the EITC depending on the number of qualifying children a taxpayer has and his or her marital status. The eligibility thresholds vary every year given that they are based in part on a parameter of the credit—the phase-out amount threshold—that is explicitly adjusted for inflation. *Table 2* shows the EITC eligibility thresholds for 2015. An EITC claimant's AGI (or earnings, if higher) must be below these thresholds for the claimant to qualify for the EITC. In 2015, these thresholds range from $14,820 for an unmarried tax filer with no qualifying child to $53,267 for a married tax filer filing jointly with three or more qualified children.

Table 2 expresses these eligibility thresholds as a percentage of the 2015 poverty guidelines. For example, the poverty guideline for a family of four in 2015 was $24,250. Families of four with income at or below this amount are considered poor. The EITC eligibility threshold of $49,974 for a married couple filing jointly with two qualifying children was more than twice (206.1%) the poverty guideline for a family of that type.

Table 2 also expresses these eligibility thresholds as a percentage of the earnings of one worker who works a minimum wage job ($7.25 per hour) 40 hours per week, 52 weeks a year ($15,080 annually). For the purposes of the calculations in *Table 2*, married EITC recipients are assumed to have the same aggregate annual earnings as unmarried recipients—$15,080. The EITC was available in 2015 to all families at this earnings level except an unmarried taxpayer with no children. The EITC was available to families with children who had earnings between 2.5 to 3.5 times the annual earnings from a minimum wage job (259.5% to 353.2% of $15,080).

Table 2. Maximum AGI to Qualify for the EITC, by Number of Qualifying Children and Filing Status in 2015

	No Qualifying Children	*One Qualifying Child*	*Two Qualifying Children*	*Three or MoreQualifying Children*
In dollars				
Unmarried	14,820	39,131	44,454	47,747
Married Filing Jointly	20,330	44,651	49,974	53,267
As a percentageof the poverty threshold				
Unmarried	125.9	245.6	221.3	196.9[a]
Married Filing Jointly	127.6	222.3	206.1	187.5[b]
As a percentageof work at the federal minimum wage, 40 hours per week, 52 weeks per year				
Unmarried	98.3	259.5	294.8	316.6
Married Filing Jointly	134.8	296.1	331.4	353.2

Source: Congressional Research Service calculations based on IRS Revenue Procedure 2014-61, Internal Revenue Code (IRC) Section 32 and the 2015 Poverty Guidelines available at https://aspe.hhs.gov/2015-povertyguidelines#guidelines.

[a] Represents the EITC AGI threshold divided by the poverty guidelines for a family of 4.

[b] Represents the EITC AGI threshold divided by the poverty guidelines for a family of 5.

PAYMENT OF THE EITC

The EITC is provided to individuals and families annually in a lump sum payment after a taxpayer files a federal income tax return.[15] It may be received in one of three ways:

1. a reduction in federal tax liability;
2. a cash payment from the Treasury if the tax filer has no tax liability, through a tax refund check; or
3. a combination of reduced federal tax liability and a refund.

The majority (87%) of the aggregate amount of the EITC—$68.1 billion in 2013—is received as a refund.[16] In other words, $59.1 billion of the EITC was received as a refund in 2013, while approximately $8.9 billion offset tax liabilities.

The EITC is taken against all taxes reported[17] on the federal individual income tax return (Form 1040) after all nonrefundable credits have been taken. On the tax form, the EITC can be found in the payments section after the lines for withholding and estimated tax payments.

The EITC benefits families when they file their income taxes. Thus, payments are generally based on the prior year's income, earnings, and family composition. That is, the EITC paid in 2016 is generally based on earnings, income, and family composition in 2015.

Interaction with Other Tax Provisions

On the tax return, the EITC is calculated after total tax liability and all nonrefundable credits. Nonrefundable tax credits, which are taken against (reduce) income tax liability, include credits for education, dependent care, savings, and the nonrefundable portion of the child credit.[18] If an EITC-eligible family has a tax liability and can use one or more of these credits, the total amount of their EITC will remain unchanged, but *how they receive the credit* will change. If nonrefundable tax credits can reduce a family's tax liability, a greater amount of their EITC will be received as a refund, and less will offset their tax liability since their tax liability is smaller.

For tax filers whose income places them in the "phase-out range" of the credit, reducing their income (all else being unchanged) will result in a larger EITC. (As illustrated in *Figure 2*, reducing income when a tax filer is in the phase-out range results in the tax filer increasing the amount of the credit they receive.) A variety of forms of income can be excluded from both AGI and earned income, reducing a taxpayer's AGI or earned income for purposes of calculating the credit. For example, pre-tax contributions to savings accounts for retirement or medical expenses are not included in either AGI or earned income. Hence, by making these contributions, EITC claimants whose pre-contribution income places them in the phase-out range of the credit will reduce their AGI or earned income for purposes of calculating the EITC and thus receive a larger credit.[19]

In contrast, for tax filers whose income places them in the "phase-in range" of the credit, reducing their income (all else unchanged) will result in a smaller EITC. (As illustrated in *Figure 2*, reducing income when a tax filer is in the phase-in range results in the tax filer reducing the amount of the credit they receive.) Generally, non-taxable income cannot be included in earned income for purposes of calculating the EITC. However, as previously discussed, service members may elect to include their nontaxable combat pay as earnings, for purposes of calculating the EITC. Generally, service members whose income (excluding their combat-pay) places them in the phase-in range will elect to include their combat pay in earned income for purposes of calculating the EITC in order to receive a larger credit.

Treatment of the EITC for Need-Tested Benefit Programs

By law,[20] the EITC cannot be counted as income in determining eligibility for, or the amount of, any federally funded public benefit program including Supplemental Nutrition Assistance Program (SNAP) food assistance, low-income housing, Medicaid, Supplemental Security Income (SSI), and Temporary Assistance for Needy Families (TANF). An EITC refund that is saved by the filer does not count against the resource limits of any federally funded public benefit program for 12 months after the refund is received.

MODIFICATIONS TO THE EITC MADE PERMANENT BY P.L. 114-113

Two temporary modifications to the EITC were enacted by the American Recovery and Reinvestment Act of 2009 (ARRA; P.L. 111-5). First, ARRA enacted a temporary larger credit for families with three or more children by creating a new higher credit rate of 45% (previously, these tax filers were eligible for a credit rate of 40%). Second, ARRA expanded marriage penalty relief by increasing the earnings level at which the credit phased out for married tax filers in comparison to unmarried tax filers with the same number of children. Before ARRA, the EITC for married tax filers would begin to phase out for earnings $3,000 (adjusted for inflation) greater than the level for unmarried recipients with the same number of children. ARRA increased this differential to $5,000 (adjusted for inflation). In 2015, this marriage penalty relief was equal to $5,520.These two changes were originally scheduled to be in effect only for 2009 and 2010. The Tax Relief, Unemployment Insurance Reauthorization, and Job Creation Act of 2010 (P.L. 111- 312) extended these ARRA provisions for two years (2011 and 2012). The American Taxpayer

Relief Act (ATRA; P.L. 112-240) extended the ARRA provisions for five more years (2013- 2017). The Protecting Americans from Tax Hikes (PATH) Act (Division Q of P.L. 114-113) made these two modifications permanent.

PARTICIPATION AND BENEFITS

The EITC was first enacted in 1975 as a temporary measure meant to encourage economic growth in the face of the 1974 recession and rising food and energy prices. It was also originally intended to "assist in encouraging people to obtain employment, reducing the unemployment rate, and reducing the welfare rolls."[21] Over time the list of EITC objectives has grown to include poverty reduction. Today the EITC is the largest need-tested, cash benefit anti-poverty program. This section first provides a historical overview of the growth of the EITC from 1975 to 2013; it then examines information on EITC participation for 2013.

Trends in Participation and EITC Benefits

When originally enacted by the Tax Reduction Act of 1975 (P.L. 94-12), the EITC was a temporary refundable tax credit in effect for 1975. For that year, 6.2 million tax filers claimed the EITC and the total EITC amount claimed was $1.25 billion (in constant 2013 dollars, this equals $5.4 billion). The credit was extended several more times on a temporary basis and made permanent by the Revenue Act of 1978 (P.L. 95-600). Legislation enacted in 1986 (P.L. 99-514), 1990 (P.L. 101-508), 1993 (P.L. 103-66), 2001 (P.L. 107-16), and 2009 (P.L. 111-5) increased the amount of the credit by changing the credit formula.

Before 1990, the credit amount was calculated as a percentage of earnings ("the credit rate") up until the earned income amount. The credit then remained at its maximum level before gradually decreasing in value as earnings increased. Legislative changes to the credit made during this time generally increased the amount of the credit in a variety of ways including increasing the credit rate, increasing the earned income amount, increasing the phase-out amount threshold, and decreasing the phase-out rate. Nonetheless, the credit amount depended on earned income.

Beginning in 1990 and more substantially in 1993, the credit formula was revised such that the credit amount varied based on earnings and, to a certain extent, the number of qualifying children. This essentially increased the credit by family size. In addition, for the first time in 1993, Congress made workers *without* qualifying children eligible for the EITC, although the credit was smaller than the credit for claimants *with* qualifying children.

In 2001, the credit formula was revised again so that it also varied based in part on marital status. As a result of this change, often referred to as "marriage penalty relief," certain married tax filers would receive a larger credit than unmarried tax filers with the same number of children. In 2009, the marriage penalty relief was expanded further and a larger credit was created for families with three or more children. These 2009 changes were extended several times and made permanent by P.L. 114-113.

Figure 3 shows the number of tax filers claiming the EITC from 1975 to 2013. *Figure 4* shows the amount of the EITC claimed on these returns, with dollar amounts adjusted for inflation to represent 2013 dollars. The figures show the effects of the legislative expansions of the EITC, with the credit experiencing growth in the late 1980s through the mid-1990s and then again in the 2000s. As shown on *Figure 4*, throughout the history of the EITC, most credits have been paid in the form of refunds, with a relatively small share of the EITC reducing regular federal income tax liability.

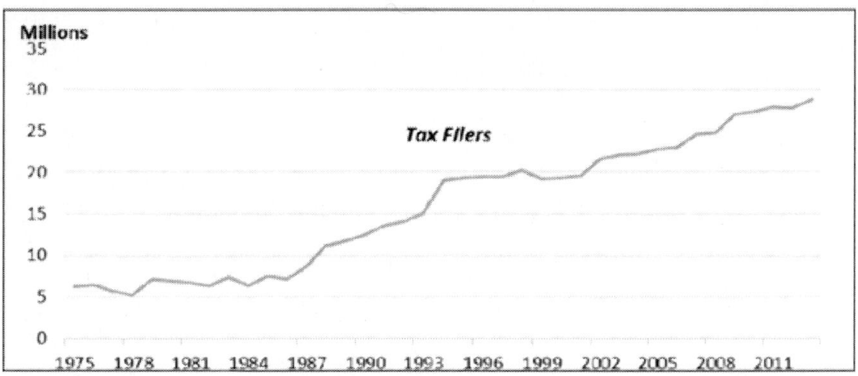

Source: Congressional Research Service. For pre-2003 data, U.S. Congress, House Committee on Ways and Means, 2004 Green Book, Background Material and Data on Programs Within the Jurisdiction of the Committee on Ways and Means, 108th Congress, 2nd session, WMCP 108-6, March 2004, pp.13-41. For 2003 and later data, Internal Revenue Service, Total File, United States, Individual Income and Tax Data, by State and Size of Adjusted Gross Income, 2003 through 2013, expanded unpublished version, Table 2.5.

Note: For a tabular display of this information, see Table A-1.

Figure 3. Number of Tax Filers Claiming the EITC: 1975 to 2013.

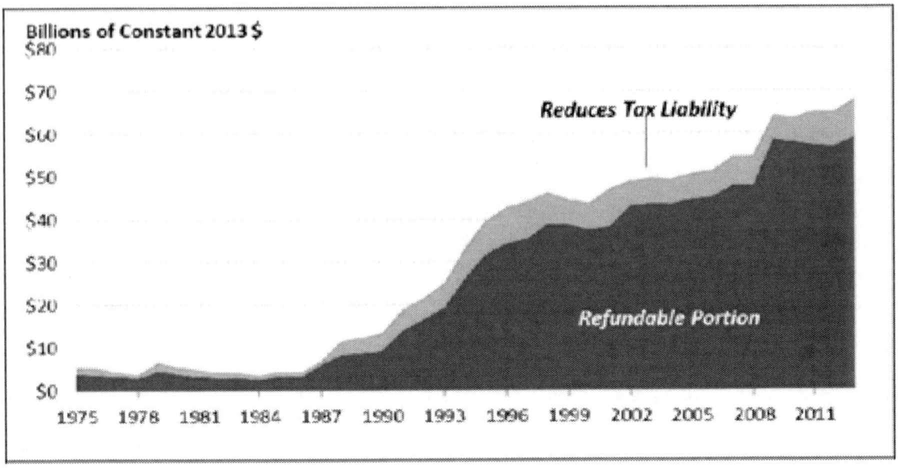

Source: Congressional Research Service. For pre-2003 data, U.S. Congress, House Committee on Ways and Means, 2004 Green Book, Background Material and Data on Programs Within the Jurisdiction of the Committee on Ways and Means, 108th Congress, 2nd session, WMCP 108-6, March 2004, pp.13-41. For 2003 and later data, Internal Revenue Service, Total File, United States, Individual Income and Tax Data, by State and Size of Adjusted Gross Income, 2003 through 2013, expanded unpublished version, Table 2.5.

Notes: Constant 2013 dollars were computed using the Consumer Price Index for all Urban Consumers (CPI-U). For a tabular display of this information, see Table A-1.

Figure 4. EITC Claimed on Federal Income Tax Returns: 1975-2013.

The growth in the total amount of EITC claimed in the late 1980s to the mid-1990s was due to not only increases in participation, but also in the average credit received by tax filers. *Figure 5* shows the average EITC claimed for 1975 to 2013, in inflation-adjusted (2013) dollars. Before the 1986 Tax Reform Act (P.L. 99-514), EITC thresholds were not indexed for inflation, and the average credit lost value each year. However, the 1986 act increased the monetary parameters of the credit for prior inflation and adjusted the threshold amounts and maximum credits annually for inflation in future years. The credit formula was also revised in 1990 and then again in 1993 such that the amount of the credit depended to a certain extent on family size. These changes resulted in an increasing average credit between the late 1980s and late 1990s. Since then, the average credit has largely maintained its real value. However, increases in the average credit amount in 2001 and 2009 were likely due to legislative changes that included larger credits for some married claimants and for families with three or more children.[22]

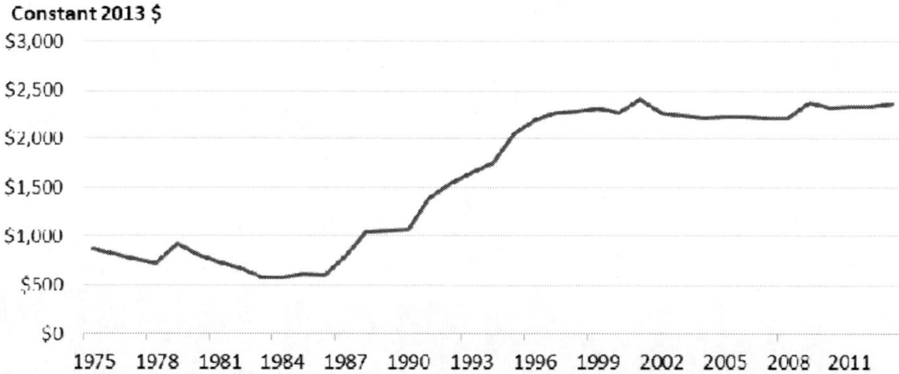

Source: Congressional Research Service. For pre-2003 data, U.S. Congress, House Committee on Ways and Means, 2004 Green Book, Background Material and Data on Programs Within the Jurisdiction of the Committee on Ways and Means, 108th Congress, 2nd session, WMCP 108-6, March 2004, pp.13-41. For 2003 and later data, Internal Revenue Service, Total File, United States, Individual Income and Tax Data, by State and Size of Adjusted Gross Income, 2003 through 2013, expanded unpublished version, Table 2.5.

Notes: Constant 2013 dollars were computed using the Consumer Price Index for all Urban Consumers (CPI-U). For a tabular display of this information, see Table A-1.

Figure 5. Average EITC Claimed: 1975 to 2013.

Participation and EITC Amounts Claimed for 2013

For 2013, $68.1 billion of the EITC was claimed on 28.8 million tax returns.

Number of Qualifying Children

Most tax filers claiming the EITC, and those who received the most EITC dollars, were families with children. *Figure 6* shows total EITC dollars claimed for 2013 by number of qualifying children. For 2013, 3% of all EITC dollars were claimed by tax filers with no qualifying children and 97% were claimed by tax filers with qualifying children. Of this 97%, 36% were claimed by tax filers with one qualifying child, 40% were claimed by tax filers with two qualifying children, and 21% were claimed by tax filers with three or more qualifying children.

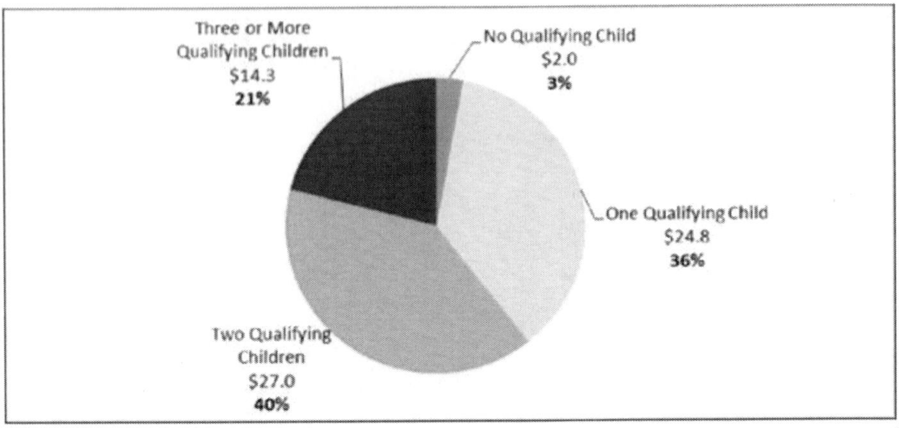

Source: Congressional Research Service, based on data from the U.S. Department of Treasury, Internal Revenue Service, SOI Tax Stats - Individual Income Tax Returns Publication 1304, Table 2.5.

Figure 6. Total EITC Dollars Claimed for 2013, by Number of Qualifying Children. (Dollars in Billions, Total EITC Claimed = $68.1 Billion.)

Though childless tax filers claimed 3% of all EITC dollars for 2013, they accounted for close to one-fourth of all tax filers that claimed the EITC. Thus, their small share of total EITC dollars reflects, in part, the lower credit amount available to childless filers.

Figure 7 shows the number of returns claiming the EITC for 2013 by number of qualifying children. *Figure 8* shows the average EITC claimed for 2013 by number of qualifying children, with the overall average amount of the EITC claimed being $2,362. The average EITC for 2013 increased with the number of qualifying children a tax filer claimed:

- The EITC was claimed by 7.3 million tax filers with no qualifying children, with an average claim of $280.
- The EITC was claimed by 10.7 million filers with one qualifying child, with an average claim of $2,326.
- The EITC was claimed by 7.4 million filers with two qualifying children, with an average claim of $3,667.
- The EITC was claimed by 3.5 million filers with three or more qualifying children, with an average claim of $4,022.

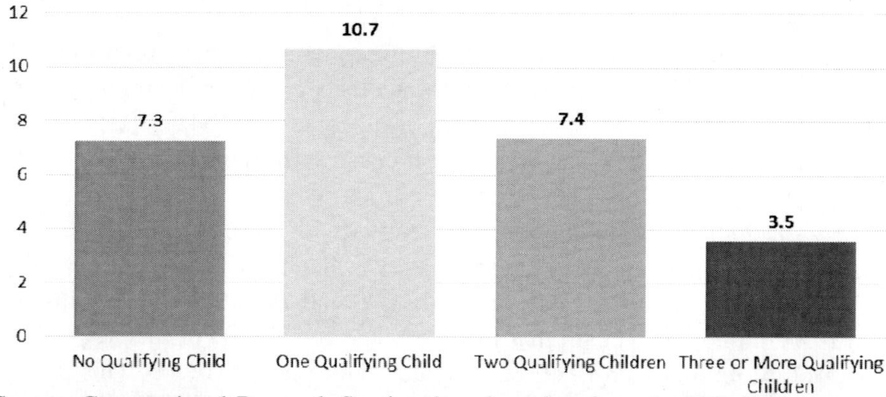

Source: Congressional Research Service, based on data from the U.S. Department of Treasury, Internal Revenue Services, SOI Tax Stats - Individual Income Tax Returns Publication 1304, Table 2.5.

Notes: Detail does not add to total because of rounding. For detail on returns claiming the EITC by AGI and number of qualifying children, see Table A-2.

Figure 7. Number of Tax Returns with EITC Claims for 2013, by Number of Qualifying Children. (Number in Millions, Total Number of Returns Claiming the EITC = 28.8 million.)

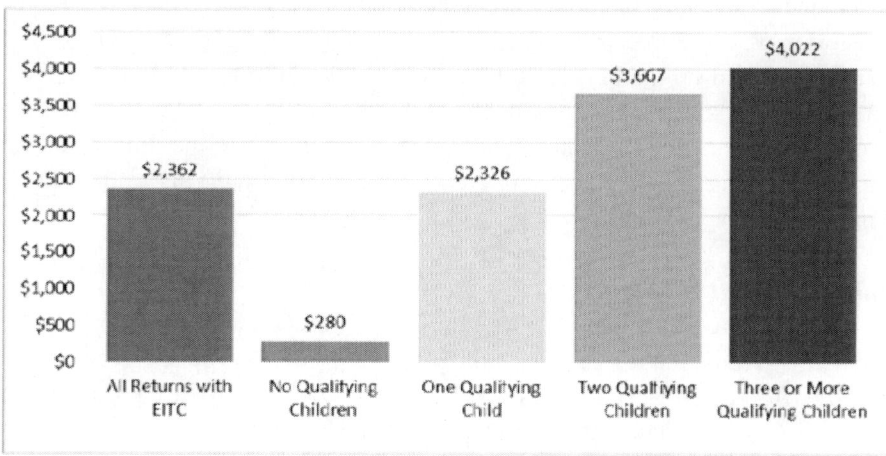

Source: Congressional Research Service, based on data from the U.S. Department of Treasury, Internal Revenue Services, SOI Tax Stats - Individual Income Tax Returns Publication 1304, Table 2.5.

Notes: For detail on returns claiming the EITC by AGI and number of qualifying children, see Table A-2.

Figure 8. Average EITC Claimed by Tax Filers in 2013, by Number of Qualifying Children.

Income Level

Though the EITC is targeted toward lower-income earners, tax filers with children may receive the EITC even with income well above the poverty level. (The federal poverty level for a family of three was $19,530 in 2013.) However, the largest EITC benefits are focused on low-income earners near the poverty line, with those with greater earnings receiving reduced benefits.

Figure 9 shows the number of tax returns with EITC claims in 2013 by adjusted gross income level. *Figure 9* shows that the most typical (modal) EITC tax return had an AGI between $10,000 and $14,999, with 6.2 million returns including an EITC in that income range for 2013. For that year, close to half of all returns with EITC claims had AGIs below $15,000. This AGI is equivalent to earnings less than the $15,080 earned by a full-time (40 hour per week) full-year (52 weeks per year) worker earning the federal minimum wage ($7.25 per hour).

Figure 9 also shows the average EITC claimed by AGI category. Average EITC benefits first increase with AGI, then decline. This outcome reflects the formula for determining the EITC, which provides an increasing credit up to a maximum amount, then ultimately a reduced credit as it is phased out above a certain income threshold (see *Table 1* and *Figure 2*). It also reflects a difference in the mix of family types claiming the EITC in the various AGI categories. For example, 70% of all filers claiming the EITC with AGIs of less than $5,000 had no qualifying children. All those claiming the EITC at AGIs above $20,000 in 2013 had qualifying children, and hence were eligible for a larger maximum EITC benefit than filers without children. For detail on returns claiming the EITC by AGI and number of qualifying children, see *Table A-2*.

Filing and Marital Status

The Internal Revenue Service does not provide data on EITC dollars claimed by filing status. The Tax Policy Center (TPC), however, projects that in 2015, 70% of all EITC dollars will be claimed by unmarried tax filers (head of household and single filing statuses), with most (60% of all EITC dollars) claimed by those filing as heads of household. (The TPC projections are likely similar to the actual amounts of the EITC claimed by filing status in 2013 and 2014, given that they are based on the same credit formula.) *Figure 10* shows projections for EITC dollars claimed by filing status for 2015.

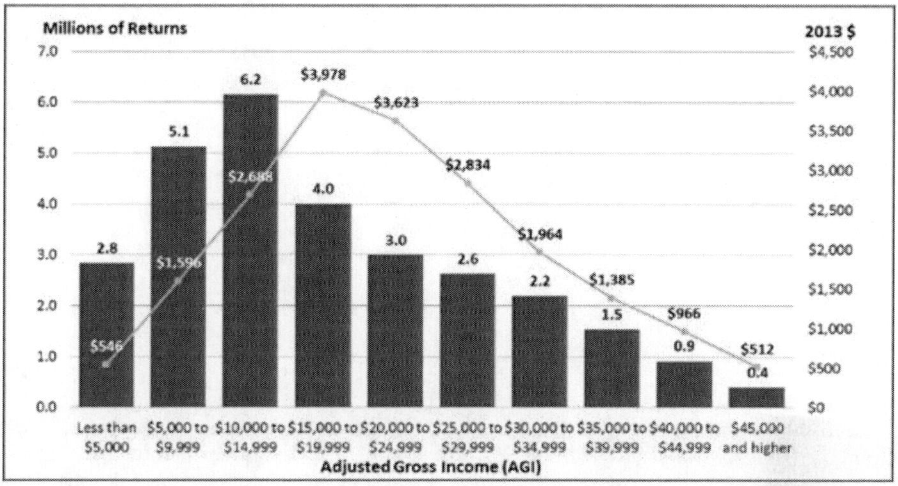

Source: Congressional Research Service, based on data from the U.S. Department of Treasury, Internal Revenue Services, SOI Tax Stats - Individual Income Tax Returns Publication 1304, Table 2.5.

Notes: For detail on returns claiming the EITC by AGI and number of qualifying children, see Table A-2.

Figure 9. Number of Returns Claiming the EITC and Average EITC Claimed for 2013, by Adjusted Gross Income. (Numbers in Millions and Dollars in 2013$)

Region

In 2013, the EITC was claimed on 19.4% of all tax returns. However, the rate at which the EITC is claimed by tax filers varies considerably by state. In 2013, the state with the highest percentage of returns claiming the EITC was Mississippi, with the credit claimed on 32.4% of all returns. In contrast, the EITC was claimed on 12.3% of all returns in New Hampshire that year.

Figure 11 provides a map showing the percentage of all tax returns claiming the EITC by state. In addition to considerable state variation, the map shows that there is a regional pattern to EITC receipt. A greater share of returns filed in certain southern states claimed the EITC than returns in other regions of the country. The EITC was claimed on the smallest percentage of returns in New England as well as some states in the northern Midwest.

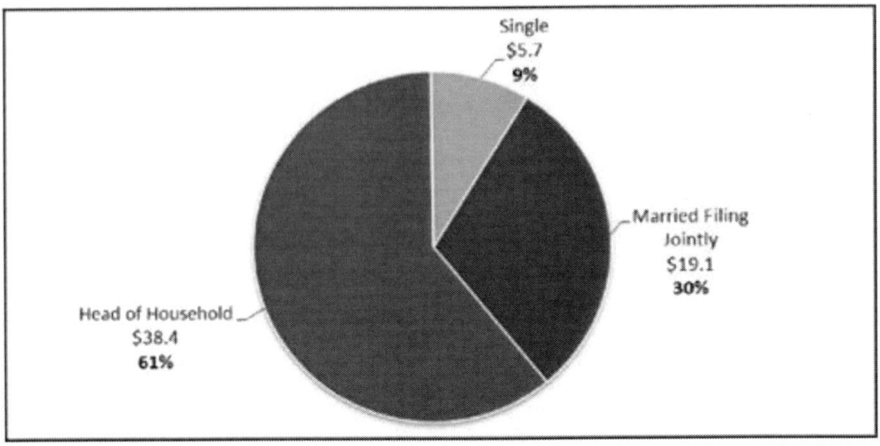

Source: Congressional Research Service, based on estimates from the Urban-Brookings Institution Tax Policy Center Table T13-0274, available at http://www.taxpolicycenter.org/numbers/index.cfm. Estimates are for tax year 2015.

Figure 10. Estimate of EITC Dollars Claimed by Marital Status, 2015. (Dollars in Billions)

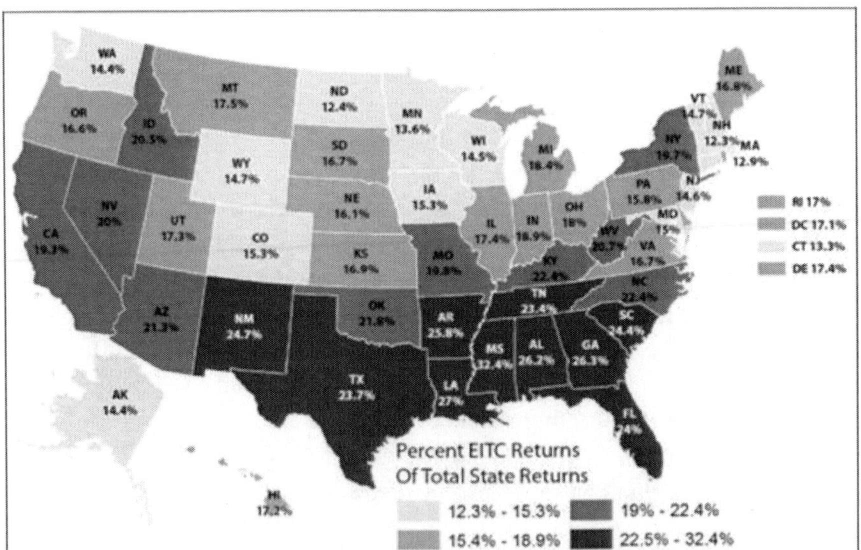

Source: Congressional Research Service, based on data from the U.S. Internal Revenue Service.

Note: For detail on EITC returns by state, see Table A-3.

Figure 11. Percentage of Tax Returns Claiming the EITC by State, 2013.

APPENDIX. ADDITIONAL TABLES

Table A-1. EITC Tax Filers and Dollars Claimed: 1975-2013

			In Millions of Nominal $	*Nominal $*	*In Millions of Constant 2013$*		*Constant2013$*
Year	Tax Filers Claiming the EITC (Millions)	Total EITC	Refunded EITC	Average EITC	Total EITC	Refunded EITC	Average EITC
1975	6.215	$1,250	$900	$201	$5,413	$3,897	$870
1976	6.473	1,295	890	200	5,302	3,644	819
1977	5.627	1,127	880	200	4,332	3,383	769
1978	5.192	1,048	801	202	3,744	2,862	722
1979	7.135	2,052	1,395	288	6,584	4,476	924
1980	6.954	1,986	1,370	286	5,615	3,873	809
1981	6.717	1,912	1,278	285	4,900	3,275	730
1982	6.395	1,775	1,222	278	4,285	2,950	671
1983	7.368	1,795	1,289	244	4,198	3,015	571
1984	6.376	1,638	1,162	257	3,673	2,605	576
1985	7.432	2,088	1,499	281	4,521	3,245	608
1986	7.156	2,009	1,479	281	4,270	3,144	597
1987	8.738	3,391	2,930	388	6,954	6,008	796
1988	11.148	5,896	4,257	529	11,610	8,383	1,042
1989	11.696	6,595	4,636	564	12,390	8,710	1,060
1990	12.542	7,542	5,266	601	13,443	9,386	1,071
1991	13.665	11,105	8,183	813	18,994	13,996	1,391
1992	14.097	13,028	9,959	924	21,632	16,536	1,534
1993	15.117	15,537	12,028	1,028	25,048	19,391	1,657
1994	19.017	21,105	16,598	1,110	33,175	26,091	1,745
1995	19.334	25,956	20,829	1,343	39,676	31,839	2,053
1996	19.464	28,825	23,157	1,481	42,798	34,382	2,199
1997	19.391	30,389	24,396	1,567	44,108	35,409	2,274
1998	20.273	32,340	27,175	1,595	46,220	38,838	2,280
1999	19.259	31,901	27,604	1,656	44,607	38,599	2,316
2000	19.277	32,296	27,803	1,675	43,691	37,613	2,266
2001	19.593	35,784	29,043	1,826	47,070	38,203	2,402
2002	21.574	37,786	33,258	1,751	48,930	43,067	2,267
2003	22.112	39,186	34,508	1,772	49,612	43,690	2,243
2004	22.270	40,024	35,299	1,797	49,359	43,532	2,216
2005	22.752	42,410	37,465	1,864	50,587	44,689	2,223
2006	23.042	44,388	39,072	1,926	51,292	45,149	2,226

Table A-1. (Continued)

			In Millions of Nominal $	*Nominal $*	*In Millions of Constant 2013$*		*Constant2013$*
Year	Tax Filers Claiming the EITC (Millions)	Total EITC	Refunded EITC	Average EITC	Total EITC	Refunded EITC	Average EITC
2007	24.584	48,540	42,508	1,974	54,537	47,759	2,218
2008	24.756	50,669	44,260	2,047	54,824	47,889	2,215
2009	27.041	59,240	53,985	2,191	64,326	58,620	2,379
2010	27.368	59,562	54,256	2,176	63,632	57,964	2,325
2011	27.912	62,906	55,350	2,254	65,148	57,323	2,334
2012	27.848	64,129	56,190	2,303	65,068	57,013	2,337
2013	28.822	68,084	59,145	2,362	68,084	59,145	2,362

Source: Congressional Research Service. For pre-2003 data, U.S. Congress, House Committee on Ways and Means, 2004 Green Book, Background Material and Data on Programs Within the Jurisdiction of the Committee on Ways and Means, 108th Congress, 2nd session, WMCP 108-6, March 2004, pp.13-41. For 2003 and later data, Internal Revenue Service, Total File, United States, Individual Income and Tax Data, by State and Size of Adjusted Gross Income, 2003 through 2013, expanded unpublished version, Table 2.5.

Notes: Constant 2013 dollars were computed using the Consumer Price Index for all Urban Consumers (CPI-U).

Table A-2. Average EITC, Number of Returns with EITC Claimed, and Total EITC Benefits for 2013, by Adjusted Gross Income

AGI	Totals	No Qualifying Children	One Qualifying Child	Two Qualifying Children	Three or More Qualifying Children
Average Credit					
Less than $5,000	$546	$218	$1,177	$1,495	$1,747
$5,000 to $9,999	1,596	413	2,761	3,095	3,418
$10,000 to $14,999	2,688	195	3,156	4,976	5,509
$15,000 to $19,999	3,978	166	3,103	5,194	5,863
$20,000 to $24,999	3,623	0	2,532	4,561	5,278
$25,000 to $29,999	2,834	0	1,807	3,606	4,422
$30,000 to $34,999	1,964	0	1,054	2,583	3,399
$35,000 to $39,999	1,385	0	519	1,637	2,485

AGI	Totals	No Qualifying Children	One Qualifying Child	Two Qualifying Children	Three or More Qualifying Children
$40,000 to $44,999	966	0	276	841	1,473
$45,000 and higher	512	0	0	338	641
Totals	2,362	280	2,326	3,667	4,022
Total Returns with EITC					
Less than $5,000	2,838,242	1,994,616	537,854	208,717	97,051
$5,000 to $9,999	5,129,061	2,673,452	1,738,302	514,983	202,326
$10,000 to $14,999	6,158,600	2,274,241	1,917,814	1,449,088	517,456
$15,000 to $19,999	4,008,364	313,299	1,772,571	1,314,389	608,103
$20,000 to $24,999	2,995,525	0	1,553,798	967,181	474,546
$25,000 to $29,999	2,630,904	0	1,326,461	870,705	433,738
$30,000 to $34,999	2,190,128	0	1,062,331	797,465	330,332
$35,000 to $39,999	1,544,531	0	598,800	614,961	330,770
$40,000 to $44,999	918,194	0	151,060	450,198	316,937
$45,000 and higher	408,239	0	0	174,039	234,199
Totals	28,821,788	7,255,608	10,658,991	7,361,726	3,545,458
Total EITC Claimed ($ in thousands)					
Less than $5,000	$1,548,386	$433,884	$632,848	$312,078	$169,575
$5,000 to $9,999	8,188,503	1,104,096	4,799,295	1,593,622	691,490
$10,000 to $14,999	16,557,395	443,096	6,053,350	7,210,511	2,850,436
$15,000 to $19,999	15,945,522	51,908	5,501,155	6,827,341	3,565,117
$20,000 to $24,999	10,851,382	0	3,934,984	4,411,631	2,504,766
$25,000 to $29,999	7,454,750	0	2,397,023	3,139,611	1,918,116
$30,000 to $34,999	4,302,376	0	1,119,570	2,060,017	1,122,789
$35,000 to $39,999	2,139,568	0	310,784	1,006,726	822,058
$40,000 to $44,999	887,310	0	41,671	378,710	466,929
Totals	68,084,087	2,032,984	24,790,680	26,999,081	14,261,337

Source: Congressional Research Service, based on data from the U.S. Department of the Treasury, Internal Revenue Services, SOI Tax Stats - Individual Income Tax Returns Publication 1304, Table 2.5.

Table A-3. Total EITC Returns and Amounts for 2013, by State

State or Area	Total Returns	Returns with EITC Claimed	Percentage of Total Returns with EITC Claimed	Total EITC Claimed ($ in thousands)	Average EITC	Percentage of EITC Refunded
U.S. Totala	146,542,500	28,487,090	19.4	$67,276,706	$2,362	86.9%

Table A-3. (Continued)

State or Area	Total Returns	Returns with EITC Claimed	Percentage of Total Returns with EITC Claimed	Total EITC Claimed ($ in thousands)	Average EITC	Percentage of EITC Refunded
Alabama	2,048,730	536,120	26.2	1,437,905	2,682	89.4
Alaska	359,140	51,800	14.4	103,910	2,006	89.6
Arizona	2,813,630	600,340	21.3	1,489,323	2,481	88.3
Arkansas	1,220,230	314,740	25.8	789,317	2,508	89.1
California	17,171,740	3,314,700	19.3	7,670,273	2,314	83.7
Colorado	2,502,950	382,850	15.3	813,304	2,124	86.8
Connecticut	1,749,600	232,190	13.3	489,158	2,107	87.0
Delaware	439,680	76,590	17.4	174,099	2,273	90.7
District of Columbia	331,050	56,650	17.1	128,373	2,266	86.5
Florida	9,316,270	2,234,430	24.0	5,352,624	2,396	85.6
Georgia	4,358,720	1,148,030	26.3	3,029,086	2,639	87.1
Hawaii	675,280	116,110	17.2	247,426	2,131	89.5
Idaho	691,620	141,990	20.5	319,091	2,247	88.3
Illinois	6,100,680	1,059,290	17.4	2,539,201	2,397	85.9
Indiana	3,047,720	575,650	18.9	1,334,191	2,318	89.2
Iowa	1,434,620	219,880	15.3	473,523	2,154	88.8
Kansas	1,325,720	223,440	16.9	507,574	2,272	89.8
Kentucky	1,886,170	423,320	22.4	980,404	2,316	88.5
Louisiana	2,004,320	541,040	27.0	1,454,045	2,688	88.7
Maine	635,870	107,120	16.8	214,425	2,002	86.0
Maryland	2,941,920	440,980	15.0	991,135	2,248	85.5
Massachusetts	3,301,030	426,950	12.9	860,908	2,016	87.6
Michigan	4,656,840	856,080	18.4	2,010,280	2,348	86.6
Minnesota	2,653,420	361,120	13.6	752,909	2,085	87.8
Mississippi	1,245,660	403,620	32.4	1,118,189	2,770	89.6
Missouri	2,743,080	542,720	19.8	1,267,252	2,335	89.1
Montana	487,640	85,180	17.5	175,065	2,055	87.9
Nebraska	880,090	141,670	16.1	317,396	2,240	89.2
Nevada	1,307,650	261,620	20.0	606,040	2,316	87.7
New Hampshire	681,760	83,680	12.3	158,584	1,895	86.1
New Jersey	4,326,880	630,100	14.6	1,415,169	2,246	85.8
New Mexico	905,730	223,560	24.7	528,239	2,363	90.2
New York	9,442,850	1,859,000	19.7	4,225,984	2,273	84.3
North Carolina	4,335,840	972,700	22.4	2,349,522	2,415	88.4
North Dakota	361,850	44,830	12.4	90,880	2,027	88.9

State or Area	Total Returns	Returns with EITC Claimed	Percentage of Total Returns with EITC Claimed	Total EITC Claimed ($ in thousands)	Average EITC	Percentage of EITC Refunded
Ohio	5,536,900	997,930	18.0	2,326,447	2,331	88.6
Oklahoma	1,630,700	355,050	21.8	853,987	2,405	88.6
Oregon	1,793,890	298,340	16.6	614,022	2,058	88.1
Pennsylvania	6,153,510	973,460	15.8	2,102,875	2,160	89.3
Rhode Island	517,840	88,210	17.0	196,572	2,228	88.2
South Carolina	2,106,060	514,460	24.4	1,266,079	2,461	89.3
South Dakota	412,660	69,090	16.7	146,089	2,114	89.8
Tennessee	2,908,080	681,750	23.4	1,671,871	2,452	87.0
Texas	11,888,890	2,813,110	23.7	7,314,092	2,600	86.2
Utah	1,196,460	206,900	17.3	473,565	2,289	88.9
Vermont	321,480	47,230	14.7	88,181	1,867	84.8
Virginia	3,834,990	640,210	16.7	1,440,634	2,250	88.2
Washington	3,293,100	473,950	14.4	997,181	2,104	88.5
West Virginia	784,420	162,160	20.7	355,150	2,190	90.9
Wisconsin	2,798,380	406,250	14.5	867,358	2,135	88.8
Wyoming	283,920	41,630	14.7	83,533	2,007	89.6
Other Areas	695,230	27,330	3.9	64,266	2,351	96.8

Source: Congressional Research Service, based on data from the U.S. Department of the Treasury, Internal Revenue Service (IRS), Individual Income and Tax Data, by State and Size of Adjusted Gross Income.

[a] Totals in this table differ slightly from total shown in Table A-2. While the figures in Table A-2 and Table A-3 are both based on data from the IRS, the data in Table A-3 includes "substitutes for returns" in which the IRS constructs tax returns for certain non-filers.

End Notes

[1] A tax filer who is claimed as a dependent on another person's tax return is ineligible for the EITC.

[2] There is an additional filing status that may claim the EITC—"qualifying widow(er) with dependent child." Generally, tax filers may file their tax return as married filing jointly in the year their spouse died. A tax filer may be eligible to use qualifying widow(er) with dependent child as his or her filing status for two years following the year his or her spouse died. This filing status entitles the tax filer to use joint return tax rates and the highest standard deduction amount (if he or she does not itemize deductions). It does not entitle the tax filer to file a joint return. The tax filer calculates the EITC using the formula for other unmarried tax filing statuses (head of household and single). The eligibility rules for this

filing status can be found on page 10 of IRS Publication 501, available at http://www.irs.gov/pub/irs-pdf/p501.pdf.

[3] The 2015 version of this form can be found at https://www.irs.gov/pub/irs-pdf/f1040sei.pdf.

[4] For more information, see http://www.irs.gov/Individuals/Special-EITC-Rules.

[5] See Internal Revenue Code (IRC) §32(c)(1)(C) and http://www.irs.gov/Individuals/EITC,-Earned-Income-TaxCredit,-Questions-and-Answers.

[6] For more information on Social Security numbers valid for work purposes, see CRS Legal Sidebar WSLG823, Social Security Number or Individual Taxpayer Identification Number for Tax Credit? That is the Question, by Emily M. Lanza, Erika K. Lunder, and Kathleen S. Swendiman and CRS Legal Sidebar WSLG723, They've Got Your Number: Who Can Get A Social Security Card, by Kathleen S. Swendiman.

[7] For more information, see CRS Report RS21732, Federal Taxation of Aliens Working in the United States, by Erika K. Lunder and http://www.irs.gov/Individuals/International-Taxpayers/Determining-Alien-Tax-Status. In addition, for the EITC, a nonresident alien may be eligible to claim the credit if they are married to a U.S. citizen or resident alien, make the election to be treated as a resident alien, and file a joint return.

[8] If an individual is the qualifying child for the purposes of the EITC of another person, that individual cannot themselves claim the EITC. For more information, see http://www.irs.gov/Individuals/EITC,-Earned-Income-TaxCredit,-Questions-and-Answers.

[9] If placed by an authorized agency or court order.

[10] Qualifying children who reside with a service member who is stationed outside the United States while serving on extended active duty with the U.S. Armed Forces are considered to reside in the United States for the purposes of the EITC.

[11] Currently, there is no Federal regulation which states that taxpayers with a qualifying child who do not claim that qualifying child for the EITC are ineligible for the credit. However, the website of the Internal Revenue Service does state that such individuals are ineligible for the childless EITC. For more information, see http://www.irs.gov/Individuals/Qualifying-Child-of-More-Than-One-Person.

[12] The tie-breaker rules are: (1) if both tax filers are parents of the child, the parent with whom the child resided the longest during the year claims the child for the EITC; (2) if the child resided with each parent for the same amount of time during the year, the parent with the highest adjusted gross income (AGI) claims the child for the EITC; (3) if only one tax filer is the parent of the child, the tax filer who is the parent claims the child for the EITC; and (4) if neither tax filer is the parent of the child, the tax filer with the highest AGI claims the child for the EITC.

[13] See IRC §32(k).

[14] The tables can be found, for 2015 returns, beginning on page 62 of the Form 1040 general instructions, at https://www.irs.gov/pub/irs-pdf/i1040gi.pdf.

[15] Before 2011, any persons with a qualified child eligible for the EITC could elect to receive advance payment of the credit through the employer's payroll withholding system by filing an eligibility certificate (Form W-5) with his or her employer. The option was little used and eliminated by P.L. 111-226.

[16] For more information, see IRS Statistics of Income, Table 2.5 at http://www.irs.gov/uac/SOI-Tax-Stats—IndividualStatistical-Tables-by-Size-of-Adjusted-Gross-Income.

[17] These taxes include the regular income tax and alternative income tax, as well as self-employment taxes. Less common taxes, like unreported Social Security and Medicare taxes and certain taxes on IRAs, are also included. For an example of these taxes, see lines 57 through 62 on the 2015 IRS Form 1040, https://www.irs.gov/pub/irs-pdf/f1040.pdf.

[18] For more information on the nonrefundable (and refundable) portion of the child tax credit, see CRS Report R41873, The Child Tax Credit: Current Law and Legislative History, by Margot L. Crandall-Hollick.

[19] In contrast, if the pre-contribution income places them in the plateau or the phase-in range, decreasing their earned income by making certain pre-tax savings contributions may either have no impact or result in a smaller credit.

[20] The Tax Relief, Unemployment Insurance Reauthorization, and Job Creation Act of 2010 (P.L. 111-312) included a provision which made tax refunds, including those resulting from the EITC, disregarded in the administration of federal programs and federally assisted programs. At the end of 2012, this provision was made permanent by the American Taxpayer Relief Act of 2012 (P.L. 112-240).

[21] U.S. Congress, Senate Committee on Finance, Tax Reduction Act of 1975, Report to Accompany H.R. 2166, 94th Cong., 1st sess., March 17, 1975, S. Report 94-36, p. 33.

[22] The increase in the value of the credit in 2009 is likely due to the changes made by the American Recovery and Reinvestment Act of 2009 (ARRA, P.L. 111-5) which expanded the credit for families with three or more children and increased marriage penalty relief.

In: The Earned Income Tax Credit
Editor: Judith L. Collins
ISBN: 978-1-63485-632-4

Chapter 2

THE EARNED INCOME TAX CREDIT (EITC): AN ECONOMIC ANALYSIS*

Margot L. Crandall-Hollick

SUMMARY

The Earned Income Tax Credit (EITC) is a refundable tax credit available to eligible workers earning relatively low wages. The EITC, enacted nearly 40 years ago, has evolved from a relatively modest tax benefit to a significant antipoverty program. In light of potential congressional interest in modifying the credit, this report reviews the economic research on the EITC. An understanding of the economic impact of the credit, as well as its limitations and potential drawbacks, may inform future legislative modifications of the credit.

When initially enacted in the 1970s, there were two major purposes of the EITC. First, the credit was meant to encourage the nonworking poor with children to enter the workforce. Second, the credit was intended to help reduce the tax burdens of working poor families with children. Some policymakers at the time worried that taxes—especially payroll taxes—would reduce poor families' take-home pay to such an extent that they would need to rely on cash welfare. In the 1990s, the purpose of the credit was expanded to include poverty reduction, with a focus on encouraging welfare recipients—generally unmarried mothers—

* This is an edited, reformatted and augmented version of a Congressional Research Service publication R44057, prepared for Members and Committees of Congress, dated February 1, 2016.

to work. At the time, the EITC was seen as a way to ensure that a full-time worker with children would not be in poverty.

As the credit has expanded and changed over time, researchers have evaluated various aspects of the credit:

- *Decisions About Working:* The EITC has encouraged single mothers to enter the workforce, but generally has had little to no impact on the number of hours they work. For example, one study found that 34% of the increase in employment among single mothers between 1993 and 1999 was due to legislative expansions of the EITC.
- *Poverty:* The EITC has had a significant impact on reducing poverty among recipients with children, but little impact among childless individuals. CRS analysis indicates that the EITC reduces unmarried and married *childless* workers' poverty rates by 0.14% and 1.39%, respectively. In comparison, the EITC reduces the poverty rates of unmarried and married workers *with children* by 14.10% and 29.38% respectively, depending on the number of children the recipient has.
- *Fairness:* The EITC has increased inequity in the tax code between those with and without children. The unequal benefit the credit provides to families with children in comparison to those without is largely due to the different objectives of the credit for these two populations. For workers with children who work full-time at a minimum wage job, the EITC was intended to ensure that the family would not be in poverty. In contrast, the smaller childless EITC was designed to help childless workers offset a gas tax increase, and not intended to lift them out of poverty.
- *Complex Rules:* The EITC's complex rules and formulas may make it difficult for taxpayers to comply with and difficult for the Internal Revenue Service (IRS) to administer. Studies indicate that EITC errors (whether intentional or unintentional) result in a relatively high proportion of EITC payments being issued incorrectly. The IRS estimates that in FY2013, 22% to 26% of EITC payments were issued improperly. The majority of the dollar amount of these errors is due to taxpayers incorrectly claiming children for the credit. In addition, the IRS may have difficulty ensuring that tax filers are in compliance with all the parameters of the EITC.

INTRODUCTION

The Earned Income Tax Credit (EITC) is a refundable tax credit available to eligible workers earning relatively low wages. Since the credit is refundable, an EITC recipient need not owe taxes to receive the benefit. Many low-income workers, especially those with children, may be eligible to receive the EITC.

The EITC, enacted 40 years ago, has evolved from a relatively modest tax benefit to a significant antipoverty program. As the credit has expanded and changed over time, researchers have evaluated various aspects of the credit, including

- how the EITC affects recipients' decision to start working (and number of hours they work);
- how the credit affects poverty rates; and
- difficulties that taxpayers have with complying with the credit's rules.

In light of potential congressional interest in modifying the credit, this report reviews the current economic research on the EITC. An understanding of the economic impacts of the credit, as well as its limitations and potential drawbacks, may inform future legislative modifications of the EITC.

This report first briefly outlines the history of the EITC, focusing on its evolution from a modest "work bonus" to a major antipoverty program. Next the report turns to an evaluation of the credit, reviewing the economic literature on how the credit has affected taxpayers' decisions to work (what economists refer to as "labor supply decisions"), how it has affected tax burdens among different taxpayers, and the complexity of administering this tax provision. This report does not provide a detailed overview of the credit.

PURPOSE AND HISTORY OF THE CREDIT

Before the EITC's enactment in 1975, cash welfare payments were the primary form of federal financial support for poor families with children. However, during the 1960s and 1970s, in the face of increasing concern over growing welfare rolls,[1] some policymakers became interested in alternative forms of aid. Economist Milton Friedman proposed a negative income tax (NIT) that would have provided a guaranteed minimum level of income administered through the tax code.[2] President Nixon, influenced by the NIT, proposed in 1969 a "family assistance plan" (FAP) that would have benefited both the working and nonworking poor with children, effectively replacing the existing cash welfare program known at the time as Aid to Families with Dependent Children (AFDC). While the Nixon plan never became law, it was twice approved by the House.[3]

Senator Russell Long, then chairman of the Senate Finance Committee, expressed interest in an alternative government assistance program which would encourage the poor to work by providing them with a "work bonus" or supplement to their wages. Senator Long's "primary objection to the NIT was that it provided its largest benefits to those without earnings"[4] and would hence discourage people from working. In contrast, Senator Long stated that his proposed "work-bonus plan" was "a dignified way" to help poor Americans "whereby the more he [or she] works the more he [or she] gets."[5]

In addition, the work-bonus plan was seen as a way to help reduce increasing payroll tax burdens. The worker's share of payroll taxes had risen from 1.5% in 1950, to 3.0% in 1960, and 4.8% in 1970.[6] During the 1960s and 1970s, there was a growing belief among policymakers that payroll taxes, as a regressive tax, especially burdened the working poor. Several antipoverty task forces also "showed that future refinancing of the Social Security system might encumber the poor even more."[7] Advocates of the work-bonus plan believed that payroll taxes reduced the poor's income to such an extent that the only way they could make ends meet was to receive welfare. According to Long, his "work bonus plan" would "prevent the social security tax from taking away from the poor and low-income earners the money they need for support of their families."[8]

In 1975, the work bonus plan was enacted on a temporary basis as part of the Tax Reduction Act of 1975 and renamed the Earned Income Tax Credit.[9] In addition to encouraging the poor to work and reducing their dependence on cash welfare, the credit was also viewed as a means to encourage economic growth in the face of the 1974 recession and rising food and energy prices.[10] Since the EITC was viewed in part as an alternative to cash welfare, it was generally targeted to the same recipients—single mothers with children.[11] (Childless poor adults would not receive the credit until the 1990s, discussed subsequently.) The credit was extended several more times on a temporary basis before being expanded and made permanent by the Revenue Act of 1978 (P.L. 95-600).[12] Making the credit permanent reflected Congress's belief "that the earned income credit is an effective way to provide work incentives and relief from income and Social Security taxes to low-income families who might otherwise need large welfare payments."[13]

In the late 1980s and 1990s, policymakers remained interested in the EITC as an antipoverty program. A *Wall Street Journal* article from 1989 described the EITC as "emerging as the antipoverty tool of choice among poverty experts and politicians as ideologically far apart as Vice President Dan Quayle and Representative Tom Downey, a liberal New York Democrat."[14] President

Bill Clinton, a champion of the EITC as a poverty-reduction tool, declared that expanding the credit would "reward the work of millions of working poor Americans by realizing the principle that if you work 40 hours a week and you've got a child in the house, you will no longer be in poverty."[15] As one scholar noted, "President Clinton's declaration completed the evolution of the EITC from Senator Long's modest 'work bonus' to a major antipoverty initiative."[16]

Before the 1990s, the EITC's structure limited its ability to reduce poverty among families of different sizes. As illustrated in *Table 1*, the EITC as originally designed did not vary by family size. Thus, as family size increased, the credit became less effective at helping a family meet its needs. The EITC was restructured to vary based on family size beginning modestly with the Omnibus Reconciliation Act of 1990 (OBRA90; P.L. 101-508) and greatly expanded by the Omnibus Reconciliation Act of 1993 (OBRA93; P.L. 103-66)[17] Specifically, the EITC was now calculated such that at any given level of earnings, the credit was one size for a taxpayer with a single child and larger for taxpayers with two or more children. For example, when OBRA93's legislative changes had fully phased in, taxpayers with one child could receive a maximum credit of $2,152, while families with two or more children could receive a maximum credit of $3,556 in 1996.[18] The 1993 bill also extended the credit to childless workers for the first time (see *Table 1)*. Unlike the expansion of the credit for workers with children, the main rationale for this "childless EITC" was not poverty reduction. Instead the credit was intended to partly offset a gasoline tax increase included in OBRA93.[19] The credit for childless workers was smaller than the credit for workers with children. It was calculated as 7.65% of the first $4,000 of earnings, for a $323 maximum credit in 1996. Notably, aside from inflation adjustments, the formula for the childless EITC has remained unchanged since OBRA93.

At the beginning of 2000, there was congressional interest among both political parties in reducing marriage penalties (although the means by which they intended to achieve this goal varied).[20] For low-income taxpayers with little or no tax liability, a marriage penalty is said to occur when a married couple receives a smaller refund than the combined refund of each partner filing as unmarried. (Marriage bonuses also arise in the U.S. federal income tax code).[21] In 2001, the Joint Committee on Taxation (JCT) identified the structure of the EITC as one of the primary causes of the marriage penalty among low-income taxpayers.[22]

In 2001, Congress chose to reduce the marriage penalty in the EITC. The Economic Growth and Tax Relief Reconciliation Act of 2001 (EGTRRA; P.L.

107-16) gradually increased the income level at which the credit phased out for married couples by $3,000 (adjusted for inflation). In 2009, ARRA temporarily increased EITC marriage penalty relief to $5,000, also adjusted for inflation. This change was originally in effect for 2009 and 2010. The increased marriage penalty relief was extended for 2011 and 2012 by the Tax Relief, Unemployment Insurance Reauthorization, and Job Creation Act of 2010 (P.L. 111-312) and further extended from 2013 until the end of 2017 by the American Taxpayer Relief Act of 2012 (P.L. 112-240; ATRA). The Protecting Americans from Tax Hikes (PATH) Act (Division Q of P.L. 114-113) made the $5,000 of EITC marriage penalty relief permanent.

CURRENT STRUCTURE OF THE EITC[23]

There are eight formulas currently in effect to calculate the EITC (four for unmarried individuals and four for married couples, depending on the number of children they have), as illustrated in *Table 2*.

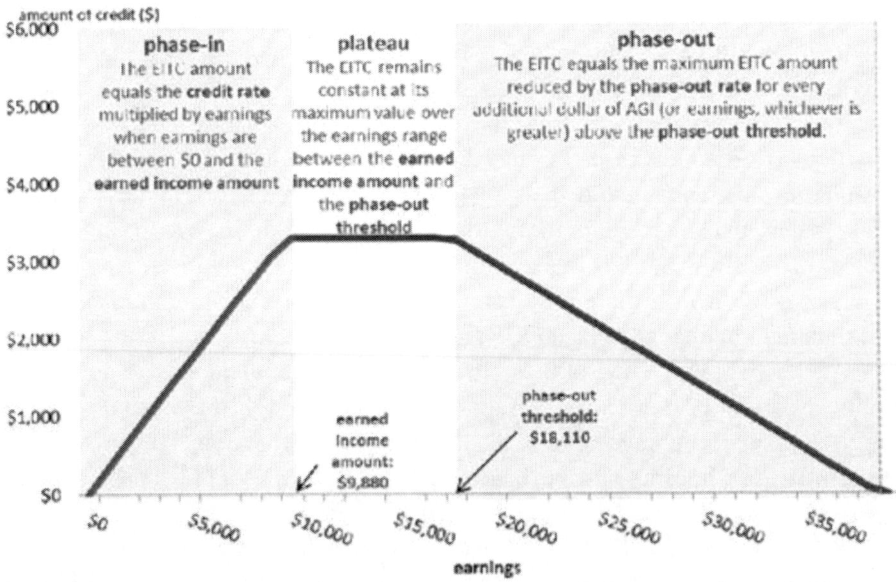

Source: Congressional Research Service based on information in IRS Revenue Procedure 2014-61 and Internal Revenue Code Section 32.

Figure 1. EITC for an Unmarried Worker with One Qualifying Child, 2015.

Table 1. Key Characteristics of the EITC Credit Formula Under Selected Laws, 1975-2009

	1975	*1978*	*1984*	*1986*	*1990*	*1993*	*2001*	*2009*
	P.L. 94-12	*P.L. 95-600*	*P.L. 98-369*	*P.L. 99-514*	*P.L. 101-508*	*P.L. 103-66*	*P.L. 107-16*	*P.L. 111-5*
Adjust Formula Parameters Such that the Amount of Credit Increases from Previous Statutory Levels *(e.g., change credit rate, earned income amount, phase-out rate or phase-out threshold, excluding marriage penalty relief)*	Enacting legislation	yes	yes	yes	yes	yes	no	yes*For families with 3+ children only*
Credit Available *Only*to Workers with Children	yes	yes	yes	yes	yes	no	no	no
Credit Amount Based on:								
Earnings*(Thecredit amount changes with earnings, equal to earnings times the credit rate in the phase-in region, the max credit amount in the plateau, and declining proportionalto the phase-out rate in the phase-out region)*	yes	yes	yes	yes	yes	yes	yes	yes
Number of Children *(The credit formula based in part on family size, with different formulas used to calculate he credit based on the number of*	no	no	no	no	yes *(credit formulas for families w/ 1 and*	yes *(credit formulas for families w/ 1 and*	yes *(credit formulas for families w/ 1 and*	yes*(credit formulas for families w/ 1,2, and 3+ children)*

Table 1. (Continued)

	1975	*1978*	*1984*	*1986*	*1990*	*1993*	*2001*	*2009*
	P.L. 94-12	*P.L. 95-600*	*P.L. 98-369*	*P.L. 99-514*	*P.L. 101-508*	*P.L. 103-66*	*P.L. 107-16*	*P.L. 111-5*
children)					*2+children)*	*2+children)*	*2+children)*	
Marital Status *(The credit phases out at a higher income level for married couples than for unmarried individuals with the same number of children. This differential is referred to as "marriage penalty relief.")*	no	no	no	no	no	no	yes*(Up to $3,000 marriage penalty relief)*	yes*($5,000 marriage penalty relief)*
Credit Available to Childless Workers	no	no	no	no	no	yes	yes	yes
Credit Adjusted Annually for Inflation	no	no	no	yes	yes	yes	yes	yes

Source: CRS analysis of P.L. 94-12, P.L. 95-600, P.L. 98-369, P.L. 99-514, P.L. 101-508, P.L. 103-66, P.L. 107-16, and P.L. 111-5.

Notes: This table does not reflect all the legislative changes that occurred to the EITC between 1975 and 2009, but instead focuses on major legislative changes to the credit formula. These include adjusting the credit for family size (including to those with no children), marital status, and for inflation, as well parameter changes (like the credit rate, earned income amount, phase-out rate and phase-out threshold).

Table 2. The Value of the EITC by Number of Qualifying Children and Marital Status, 2015

number of qualifying children	0	1	2	3 or more
unmarried tax filers(single and head of household filers)				
credit rate	7.65%	34%	40%	45%
earned income amount	$6,580	$9,880	$13,870	$13,870
maximum credit amount	$503	$3,359	$5,548	$6,242
phase-out threshold	$8,240	$18,110	$18,110	$18,110
phase-outrate	7.65%	15.98%	21.06%	21.06%
income when credit = 0	$14,820	$39,131	$44,454	$47.747
married tax filers(married filing jointly)				
credit rate	7.65%	34%	40%	45%
earned income amount	$6,580	$9,880	$13,870	$13,870
maximum credit amount	$503	$3,359	$5,548	$6,242
phase-out threshold	$13,750	$23,630	$23,630	$23,630
phase-outrate	7.65%	15.98%	21.06%	21.06%
income when credit = 0	$20,330	$44,651	$49,974	$53,267

Source: IRS Revenue Procedure 2014-61 and Internal Revenue Code (IRC) Section 32.

For any claimant, the credit has three value ranges that vary by income as illustrated in *Figure 1*. First, the credit value increases to its maximum value from the first dollar of earnings until earnings reach the "earned income amount." Over this "phase-in range" the credit value is equal to the credit rate multiplied by earnings. When earnings are between the "earned income amount" and the "phase-out threshold"—referred to as the "plateau"—the credit amount remains constant at its maximum level. For each dollar over the "phase-out threshold," the credit is reduced by the phase-out rate until the credit equals zero. This final range of income over which the credit falls in value is referred to as the "phase-out range."

How to Calculate the EITC

The following examples illustrate how to calculate the EITC for an unmarried taxpayer with one qualifying child at varying levels of income, as illustrated in *Figure 1* and using the parameters in *Table 2*. (For simplicity, these examples assume that earned income equals adjusted gross income (AGI).)

Earned Income of $9,000: The taxpayer's income places them in the *phase-in range* of the credit. Their credit equals the credit rate multiplied by their earned income. In this case, 34% x $9,000 or $3,060.

Earned Income of $15,000: The taxpayer's income places them in the *plateau* of the credit. Their credit equals the maximum amount of the credit or $3,359.

Earned Income of $30,000: The taxpayer's income places them in the *phase-out range* of the credit. The maximum value of the credit ($3,359) is reduced by 15.98 cents for every dollar above the phase-out threshold of $18,110. When the taxpayer's earned income was $30,000, the credit would fall by $11,890 ($30,000 minus $18,110) multiplied by 15.98 cents or $1,900. In other words the credit would equal $1,459 ($3,359 minus $1,900).

EVALUATION OF THE CREDIT

Generally, economists evaluate tax policies—including the EITC—through three different lenses: how the tax provision affects taxpayers' behavior ("efficiency"), how the tax provision affects tax burdens ("equity" or "fairness," which necessitates defining fairness), and the complexity of administering the tax provision ("administration"). A provision may be seen differently through these lenses. For example, a tax provision may simplify the tax code (improve administration), but result in an undesirable behavior (reduce efficiency). The following sections review the research on the EITC in terms of its impact on efficiency, equity, and administration.

Efficiency: How Has the Credit Affected Recipients' Decisions to Work?

Most economic research on the EITC has focused on how the credit affected the work decisions of the original target population of the EITC—unmarried mothers. Indeed unmarried claimants with children remain the majority of EITC recipients and receive the majority of EITC dollars.[24] More recently, as the goals and structure of the credit have changed, there has also been some interest in how the credit affects the labor force decisions of married couples. A smaller body of research has examined the impact the EITC has on married secondary earners with children, generally assumed to be women.[25] Research tends to examine either the impact that the credit had on a population's decision to start working ("work force participation") or on their decision to work a different number of hours. In some cases, research looks at both of these labor supply decisions. A detailed overview of the economic theory of the labor supply effect (decision to work and number of hours worked) of the EITC is provided in the *Appendix*.

Workforce Participation of Unmarried Workers

Studies indicate that the EITC has a positive effect on the labor force participation of single mothers.[26] These studies generally examine how significant legislative expansions of the EITC influenced previously nonworking single mothers' decisions to enter the workforce.[27] For example, one study found that the creation of a larger credit for unmarried individuals with two or more children in the early-1990s resulted in a sharp increase in employment among single mothers.[28] Another study found that 34% of the increase in employment among single mothers between 1993 and 1999 was due to legislative expansions of the EITC.[29] Other research found that "60% of the 8.7 percentage point increase in annual employment of single mothers between 1984 and 1996 is attributable to the EITC with its expansion."[30] In addition to encouraging many single mothers to enter the workforce, the EITC also played a role in reducing welfare caseloads. Research evaluating the interaction between welfare policy and the EITC in the 1990s found that the EITC had a substantial effect in reducing new entries into the cash welfare program.[31] In other words, many single mothers chose to work, and receive the EITC, rather than apply for welfare.

Workforce Participation of Married Workers

In comparison to unmarried workers, research is less conclusive as to the impact of the EITC on married secondary earners' decisions to start working. Some empirical evidence suggests that the EITC has caused a small percentage of married mothers to stay out of the labor force. One study, which assumed that married secondary earners were women, found that "the 1993 EITC expansion led to a one percentage point reduction in the participation rate of married mothers."[32] Another study found that legislative changes that expanded the EITC resulted in some married women choosing not to work.[33] Couples may decide, for example, that one spouse's EITC is sufficiently large to allow the other spouse to stay out of the workforce and instead raise children. These couples could determine that having two earners would not only reduce their EITC, but may also increase the cost of other expenses, like child care, ultimately lowering their disposable income. However, more recent research has found that among married women, the EITC has had a negligible effect on labor force participation.[34]

If the EITC is discouraging some secondary earners from working it would effectively be "subsidizing the lower earning partner in a married couple to stay home."[35] Whether that is desirable from a policy perspective depends on policymakers' goals with respect to married couples with children.

Hours Worked of Unmarried Workers

Among unmarried workers, research on the impact of the EITC on hours worked is not necessarily consistent with theoretical predictions. Fundamental to the *theoretical* impact of the EITC on hours worked are the concepts of "income" and "substitution" effects. These effects can help economists predict how a worker will behave in response to a policy like the EITC.

For example, in the phase-in region of the credit, the EITC increases the compensation per hour worked (or the "marginal return to work"). For an unmarried worker with one child, $1 of wages pre-EITC will yield $1.34 of wages postEITC. This additional income makes the worker feel richer for the same amount of work. If the worker has an income target ("I need to make $200 this week"), an increase in wages from the EITC means they can work *less* to achieve the *same* level of income. Economists refer to this as the "income effect" of the EITC. At the same time, an increase in the marginal return to work means that "not working" or "leisure" implicitly costs more in terms of foregone wages. Returning to the example of the unmarried worker with one child, not working now costs the individual $1.34 in foregone income instead of $1. Hence, the individual will consume less leisure, and work more. Economists refer to this as the "substitution effect" of the EITC. Hence, if a worker is in the phase-in range of the credit, the impact of the EITC is theoretically ambiguous. The income effect implies they work less, while the substitution effect implies they work more.

However, most EITC recipients' income places them in the *plateau* or *phase-out* region of the credit, where the economic framework of income and substitution effects suggest workers will be encouraged to reduce the hours they work.[37]

Basic Economic Theory of How Taxation Affects Labor Supply

Economists often use the theoretical framework of "income" and "substitution" effects to assess the impact income tax policies—including the EITC—have on labor supply (the decision to work and the number of hours worked). Underlying this framework is the assumption that when a worker is deciding whether to work more or work less, they are ultimately choosing between two goods: leisure (i.e., hours of *not working*) and consumption (after-tax dollars they can spend on goods).

Substitution effect: When wages increase, the cost of leisure also increases, since the cost of leisure is implicitly the foregone wages from not working.[36] Given the laws of supply and demand (as the price of a good rises, consumption falls and vice versa), a worker will "consume less leisure" and hence work more according to the substitution effect.

Income Effect: As wages increase, a worker will have more income and consume more of all goods, including leisure. In other words, an individual will *work less*.

The ultimate impact a wage increase has on hours worked depends on which effect is greater. If the substitution effect is larger, an individual will work more hours as their wages increase. If the income effect is larger, an individual will work fewer hours as their wages increase.

- Plateau: If taxpayers' income places them in the plateau region, they would receive the same amount of the EITC regardless of the number of hours worked. In this region, the EITC neither increases nor decreases hourly wages, and hence has no substitution effect. But since workers still receives the credit, then according to the income effect, they will work fewer hours. Hence, overall, economic theory suggests workers will cut back on hours worked.
- Phase-out: If recipients' income places them in the phase-out region of the credit, the value of the credit falls for each additional hour worked, and according to the substitution effect, "leisure" became less costly, and so workers work less. In addition, in the phase-out region, the credit is still available, and so according to the income effect, workers would also be encouraged to work fewer hours. Hence, overall, economic theory suggests that both the income and substitution effects will encourage workers to cut back the hours they work.

Yet, despite the theoretical predictions, most of the empirical evidence indicates the EITC has "had little effect on the number of hours they work."[38] As one study stated,

> ...theory implies that the EITC will decrease hours worked among those already working because most recipients are on the plateau or phase-out portion of the credit schedule. However, recent hours worked patterns for EITC eligible individuals do not appear to fit this second prediction. Hours and weeks worked by likely recipient groups have not fallen. [39]

There are several explanations as to why the EITC may have had little impact on the *number of hours* unmarried parents work. Chief among them is that the complexity and timing of the EITC limits its work incentive effect. Taxpayers may not understand the complex relationship between the credit's value and the worker's earnings, complexity that is likely compounded by receiving the credit the year *after* employment decisions are made. In addition, some experts suggest that instead of responding to the marginal impact that work has on their EITC amount (and overall tax liability), tax filers instead make their decision about how much they will work based on their average tax rate (their total taxes or refund divided by their total income).[40] The impact of additional earnings on average tax rates is generally lower than its impact on marginal tax rates, which may also account for the limited impact of the EITC on hours worked. Finally, workers in low-wage jobs may not have the flexibility to alter the number of hours they work, even if they would like to.

Recent Research

More recent research has provided a more complex picture of taxpayer behavior with respect to the EITC, behavior that might not be apparent in the previous analyses of aggregate data. Specifically, it is possible that in certain circumstances a worker may adjust their income level (including by adjusting hours worked) to maximize their credit. To understand this finding, it is important to remember that there are two inflection or "kink" points in the EITC schedule: at the earned income amount and at the phase-out threshold, as illustrated in *Figure 1*. The earned income amount is the *lowest* earnings level at which the credit reaches its maximum amount. The phase-out threshold is the *highest* earnings level at which the credit remains at its maximum amount. Recent research has examined whether taxpayers "bunch" around these inflection points. In other words, do taxpayers tend to earn the exact amount of money needed to get the largest credit?

One study found "clear evidence of bunching around the first kink point of the EITC—the point at which the credit reaches its maximum level."[41] In addition, bunching tended to increase over time, suggesting taxpayers were learning about the structure of the EITC. This effect however was concentrated among the self-employed—who "tend to have a substantial ability to manipulate their earnings (both by reducing hours or reducing reported earnings)."[42] No bunching effect was found among EITC recipients with only wage income and the authors did not report evidence of bunching around the second kink point of the EITC. However, these results did indicate that some self-employed individuals were aware of the EITC formula, and how it varied by earnings. Using high rates of "self-employed bunching" as a proxy for "high knowledge" about the structure of the EITC, a subsequent study focusing on wage earners found that EITC claimants who live in "high knowledge" neighborhoods tended to have wage earnings concentrated in the EITC plateau.[43] Crucially, the authors noted that

> the welfare consequences of the EITC depend on whether the higher concentration of earnings around the refund-maximizing plateau of the EITC schedule comes from increased earnings for those who would have been in the phase-in region or reduced earnings for those who would have been in the phase-out region.[44]

Does the EITC Affect Individuals' Decisions to Marry?

Some policymakers are interested in the impact of the EITC on unmarried workers' decision to marry, especially since many married EITC recipients may receive a smaller EITC as a married couple than their combined EITCs as two single tax filers. A smaller EITC for married couples (known as a "marriage penalty") could discourage cohabitating couples from marrying.[45] (Importantly, certain couples can receive a marriage bonus from the EITC).

For example, in 2014, two single parents, each with one child and earned income of $15,000, would receive an EITC of $3,305 each for a total EITC of $6,610. If they married, their combined income would be $30,000, and with two children, their EITC would be $4,041.[46] The EITC marriage penalty for this couple would be $2,659.

While limited, research indicates that the EITC's effects on marriage patterns are small and ambiguous.[47]

Assuming no changes in wage rates, this would imply workers would adjust the number of hours they work to maximize the credit. The authors found that the majority of the clustering effect in the plateau region was from workers whose income originally placed them in the phase-in region working *more* hours, rather than from those in the phase-out region working *fewer* hours. These studies suggest that low-income workers may respond to the EITC by increasing hours worked.

However, this newer research still does not explain why the EITC apparently *does not* lead to an overall reduction in hours worked among workers whose income places them in the phase-out range, even though economic theory suggests otherwise. As Hoynes states with respect to workers whose income places them in the phase-out region of the credit "we expect hours to decrease ... the literature has failed to find a consistent negative impact of the EITC on hours worked. This, I think, is a bit of a puzzle."[48] One possible theory is that workers in the phase-in range are part-time workers and can increase their hours in response to the EITC, whereas workers in the phase-out range are likely full-time workers who might not have the option to cut back their hours.

Hours Worked of Married Workers

With respect to married couples, research focusing on the secondary earner found that the EITC does tend to result in a slight reduction of hours worked among these workers. One study found that EITC expansions resulted in a 0.57% to 4.37% reduction in hours worked among married women,[49] while another study found a similar reduction of 1% to 4% of hours worked among married women.[50]

Decisions to Work of Childless Workers

Finally, studies have not focused on the labor supply effects of the EITC for childless workers. One reason may be because the EITC for childless workers was enacted after the credit for workers with children and unlike the credit for workers with children, the childless EITC formula was never expanded. As previously discussed, many studies of the EITC looked at how legislative *expansions* of the credit for workers with children affected their labor force decisions. The EITC for childless workers has effectively remained unchanged from its 1993 formula—except for annual inflation adjustments. In addition, the EITC for childless workers is likely too small to encourage workers to work at a low-wage job, especially on a full-time basis. For example, a childless worker working full time at a minimum wage job[51] (40 hours a week, 50 weeks a year) would receive a $7 credit in 2014. In contrast, a single parent with just one child working full time at a minimum wage job would receive a $3,305 credit.

Equity: How Has the Credit Affected Poverty Rates and Tax Burdens?

When examining the impact the EITC has on fairness or equity, research has tended to focus on how the credit affects poverty rates and tax burdens among different groups of recipients. The EITC has had a significant impact on reducing poverty among recipients with children, but little impact among childless individuals. In addition, the EITC has increased inequity in the tax code between those with and without children.

Poverty Reduction

The EITC is one of the federal government's largest antipoverty programs,[52] reflecting a trend toward reducing poverty through the tax code.[53] The official poverty measure, however, is unable to capture the antipoverty impact of the EITC. The official poverty measure is calculated by comparing an individual's or family's resources, measured as pre-tax cash income (hence excluding the EITC), to a poverty threshold, roughly equal to three times the cost of spending on the U.S. Department of Agriculture's Economy Food Plan. If an individual's or family's resources are less than their applicable threshold, the individual or family is counted as poor.[54]

New experimental poverty measures that include government benefits like the EITC provide evidence of such programs' antipoverty effects. The U.S. Census Bureau found that when government tax and transfer programs were included in a broader measure of poverty, refundable tax credits were estimated to reduce poverty by three percentage points. This compares to a 1.6 percentage-point reduction for food assistance (known as SNAP or the Supplemental Nutrition Assistance Program) and a 0.2 percentage-point reduction for welfare (known as TANF or the Temporary Assistance for Needy Families).[55] Although this analysis includes both the EITC and refundable portion of the child tax credit, the EITC is the largest refundable tax credit targeted to the poor, and previous research indicates that most of the antipoverty impact of refundable tax credits can be attributed to the EITC.[56]

The antipoverty effects of the EITC are not uniform across different types of households and tax filers. *Figure 2* illustrates how pre-tax income of workers at the federal poverty level (FPL)[57] changes after subtracting taxes owed (including payroll taxes) and adding back the EITC. Under the current federal income tax, married and unmarried childless workers with pre-tax income at the FPL tend to see their income remain below the poverty line after taxation, *even when including the EITC*. In contrast, married and unmarried workers with children whose pre-tax income is at the FPL will have post-tax income above the FPL because the EITC is greater than their payroll tax liability. Many poor tax filers, especially those with children, do not generally owe federal *income* tax.[58]

In addition, as illustrated in *Table 3*, poor childless workers tend to have very low incomes, with 43% to 47% of those in poverty in extreme poverty, meaning their incomes are below 50% of the FPL. Although poor childless workers tend to be extremely poor, and poorer than their peers with children, childless workers receive a maximum EITC that is significantly smaller than the credit received by workers with children. Hence, the EITC reduces unmarried and married childless workers' poverty rates by 0.14% and 1.39%, respectively, in comparison to rates for workers with children that are at least 15 times larger (see *Table 3*).

As illustrated in *Table 3*, the EITC reduces poverty rates more for married parents than for single parents. The data also indicate, however, that a major factor in this difference may be that poor single parents are generally much more impoverished than their married peers. Hence, for poor single parents, the EITC may be too small to push them over the poverty threshold.

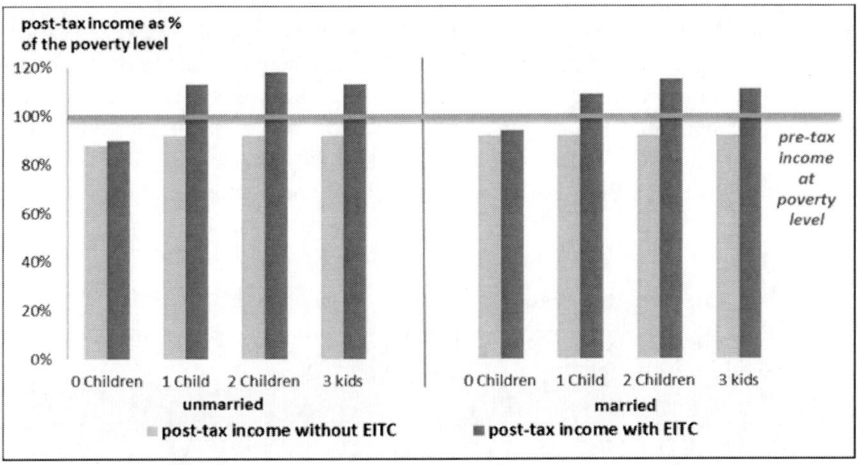

Source: CRS calculations.

Notes: The term “tax” includes federal income tax and the employee’s share of payroll taxes. Other tax credits that recipients may be eligible for, like the child tax credit, are not included.

Figure 2. Effects of Taxes and EITC on Taxpayers at Poverty Level, 2014.

Table 3. The Impact of the EITC on Poverty Rates, 2012 (by marital status and number of related children under the age of 18)

Family Characteristics	Percentage of Families in Poverty Using an Alternative Measure of Income		Percentage Change in Poverty Rates from the EITC	Addendum: Percentage ofPoor in Extreme Poverty (below 50% ofthe official federal poverty line)	
Marital Status	Number of Related Children Under 18 in the Family		EITC Excluded from Income	EITC Included in Income	
Single	0	22.29%	22.26%	-0.14%	47.41%
1	29.11%	24.74%		-15.02%	44.59%
2	33.97%	28.31%		-16.65%	41.75%
3	48.03%	41.26%		-14.10%	41.68%
Married	0	4.44%	4.38%	-1.39%	43.26%
1	5.27%	4.17%		-20.89%	36.06%
2	6.10%	4.46%		-26.86%	30.55%
3	10.04%	7.09%		-29.38%	29.69%

Source: CRS analysis of the 2013 Current Population Survey.[59]

Notes: The poverty rates in this table—both pre- and post-EITC—do not reflect the official poverty rate calculations. The poverty rates are calculated by comparing a family's resources to the official poverty threshold. For the purposes of this analysis, a family's resources include government benefits (like Social Security, food assistance, housing assistance, health benefits) net of taxes paid and expenses associated with work, like child care. The EITC is then included in one measure of resources, but excluded in the other. Both measures of resources are then compared with the official poverty threshold to determine if the individual or family is poor. This data illustrates several key aspects of the antipoverty effectiveness of the EITC based on marital status and number of children.

Tax Burdens

Tax burdens are the percentage of a taxpayer's income that is paid in taxes. In this report, the terms tax burdens, effective tax rates, and average tax rates are used interchangeably.

Tax Burdens by Income

The EITC changes the distribution of the tax burden across taxpayers at different income levels. Data from the Tax Policy Center (TPC), summarized in *Table 4*, illustrate the impact of the EITC on the effective tax rates paid by tax units in different income classes. TPC estimates that in 2013, the EITC lowered the average tax rates for tax units with income below $75,000, providing the greatest benefit to those with income between $10,000 and $20,000. Notably, the TPC estimates show that the EITC does not result in the poorest tax units paying the lowest average tax rates, as many tax units in the lowest income class are ineligible for the EITC or only eligible for a small EITC.[60]

Table 4. Federal Tax Rates with and Without the EITC, 2013

Tax Units' Cash Income Level	Average Federal Tax Rate		Average Decrease in Federal Tax Liability from Credit	Percent of Tax Units Who Receive the Benefit	Share of Total Value of EITC
	Without EITC	With EITC			
Less than $10,000	7.6%	3.9%	$219	26.7%	4.2%
$10,000-$20,000	5.7%	1.8%	$583	29.3%	20.8%
$20,000-$30,000	7.9%	4.2%	$908	28.1%	27.0%
$30,000-$40,000	9.7%	7.4%	$818	27.3%	20.2%
$40,000-$50,000	11.2%	9.7%	$665	26.0%	14.2%
$50,000-$75,000	13.2%	12.7%	$306	16.8%	11.5%

Tax Units' Cash Income Level	Average Federal Tax Rate		Average Decrease in Federal Tax Liability from Credit	Percent of Tax Units Who Receive the Benefit	Share of Total Value of EITC
	Without EITC	With EITC			
$75,000-$100,000	15.0%	15.0%	$40	3.0%	0.9%
$100,000-$200,000	17.6%	17.6%	$3	0.1%	0.1%
$200,000+	22.6%	22.6%	$0	0.0%	0.0%

Source: Tax Policy Center, Table T13-0220, http://www.taxpolicycenter. org/numbers/Content/PDF/T13- 0220.pdf.

Notes: Tax units in each income class include both those eligible and ineligible for the EITC. Cash income includes wages and salaries, investment (taxable dividends, realized net capital gains) and business income, as well as government transfer payments (Social Security, SSI, veterans benefits), employee contributions to tax-deferred retirement savings plans, and business income or loss. In addition, it includes both filing and non-filing units but excludes those that are dependents of other tax units. Tax units with negative adjusted gross income are excluded from their respective income class but are included in the totals. For a description of expanded cash income, see http://www.taxpolicycenter.org/TaxModel/income.cfm.

What is a "tax unit"?

When economists analyze the tax code or tax provisions, their analysis often focuses on the impact of tax policy on a "tax unit." A tax unit is defined as either an individual, or in the case of those filing a married joint return, a married couple, and all the dependents of the individual or married couple.

For the purposes of the analysis of tax burdens in this report only, "tax units" will sometimes be used interchangeably with the terms "families" or "households." However, the technical definition of "families" and "households" used by other government agencies like the Census Bureau may result in tax units and families and households differing.[61]

Tax Burdens by Family Structure

Economists also evaluate how tax provisions affect the tax burdens of different families. In effect, they evaluate the tax burdens of "equivalent" families or families that have the same standard of living. These families will have the same "ability-topay" a tax. Tax policies that result in families with the same "ability-to-pay" having the same tax burden are referred to as horizontally equitable by economists.

A family's ability to pay will be affected by the size and composition of the family. As families increase in size, they tend to need additional income to have the same standard of living as smaller families. However, the amount of additional resources will not be the same for each additional family member. For example, one study found that by using a commonly accepted formula—called an "equivalence scale"—to adjust for family size, a family composed of one individual with a cash income of $10,000, was equivalent to (i.e., had the same standard of living) as a family with two members and a cash income of $14,142, a family with three members and cash income of $17,321, and a family of four and cash income of $20,000.[62]

Using an equivalence scale developed to determine poverty thresholds for families of different sizes,[63] one study concluded that the EITC resulted in tax rates among low-income tax filers that were horizontally inequitable.[64] For example, when comparing families whose incomes were equivalent to $10,000 (what the researchers called "the reference income level"),[65] the authors found that

> At a $10,000 reference income, all effective tax rates are negative, and the rates range from -1.47 percent for a married couple with no children to -39.21 percent for a head-ofhousehold return with two children, a difference of more than a third of income.[66]

Using equivalence scales developed by the Census Bureau,[67] and calculating 2015 effective tax rates based on these income levels and family compositions, more recent analysis indicates that horizontal inequity also exists at higher income levels, as illustrated in *Table 5*. A major factor in this horizontal inequity among low-income tax filers is the larger EITC credit for families with children, which results in "dramatic differences between families with and without children."[68,69] As incomes rise to around $25,000, the variation in effective tax rates falls among equivalent families, as fewer tax filers are eligible for the EITC or are eligible for a smaller EITC due to the phase out of the credit. In addition, the child tax credit further increases horizontal inequity between those with and without children. This has led researchers to conclude that "the clearest change that would increase horizontal equity ... is a larger EITC for single workers and childless couples."[70]

Table 5. Effective Tax Rates for Families with the Same Reference Income, 2015

	Single	Married 0 Children	Married1 Child	Married 2 Children	Married 3 Children	HOH1 Child	HOH2 Children	HOH3 Children
Reference Income Level: $10,000for a Married Couple with No Children								
Equivalent Income	$7,071	$10,000	$13,429	$15,257	$16,995	$10,670	$12,668	$14,538
Effective Tax Rate (w/o CTC)	-7.11%	-5.03%	-25.01%	-36.36%	-36.73%	-31.48%	-40.00%	-42.93%
Effective Tax Rate (w/CTC)	-7.11%	-5.03%	-32.46%	-48.42%	-49.08%	-40.85%	-51.45%	-54.84%
Effective Tax Rate (w/CTC and payroll)	0.54%	2.62%	-24.81%	-40.77%	-41.43%	-33.20%	-43.80%	-47.19%
Reference Income Level: $15,000for a Married Couple with No Children								
Equivalent Income	$10,607	$15,000	$20,143	$22,886	$25,493	$16,005	$19,001	$21,807
Effective Tax Rate (w/o CTC)	-2.65%	-2.61%	-16.68%	-24.24%	-22.64%	-20.99%	-27.90%	-24.78%
Effective Tax Rate (w/CTC)	-2.65%	-2.61%	-21.64%	-32.98%	-34.41%	-27.23%	-38.42%	-37.72%
Effective Tax Rate (w/CTC *and* payroll)	5.00%	5.04%	-13.99%	-25.33%	-26.76%	-19.58%	-30.77%	-30.07%
Reference Income Level: $25,000for a Married Couple with No Children								
Equivalent Income	$17,678	$25,000	$33,572	$38,143	$42,489	$26,676	$31,669	$36,344
Effective Tax Rate (w/o CTC)	4.17%	1.76%	-2.42%	-3.83%	-2.83%	-3.76%	-5.03%	-3.40%
Effective Tax Rate(w/CTC)	4.17%	1.76%	-5.40%	-9.07%	-9.89%	-7.51%	-11.34%	-11.65%
Effective Tax Rate (w/CTC *and* payroll)	11.82%	9.41%	2.25%	-1.42%	-2.24%	0.14%	-3.69%	-4.00%

Source: CRS calculations using a three-parameter “equivalence” scale used to calculate equivalent families for the supplemental poverty measure. For more information see Kathleen Short, The Supplemental Poverty Measure: 2013, U.S. Census Bureau, Current Population Reports, October 2014, p. 19. Effective tax rates calculated using NBER’s TAXSIM model for tax year 2015.

Notes: HOH: Head of Household filing status. CTC: The child tax credit. Negative tax rates indicate that that the tax filer receives a refund. These rates are calculated as the total tax divided by income. For the calculations, all income is assumed is assumed to be wage income, the taxpayer taxes no above-the line deductions, and the taxpayer takes the standard deduction and appropriate number of personal exemptions when calculating their taxable income. With respect to the number of children, all are assumed to be under 17, and hence with respect to the child tax credit, eligible for that credit. Payroll taxes are calculated as 7.65% of income.

While the effective tax rates of "equivalent families" provided in *Table 5* depend in part on the equivalence scale used, research indicates that horizontal inequities will still exist—though to different degrees—even when assumptions used to construct equivalence scales differ.[71]

Simplicity and Administrability: Are the EITC Eligibility Rules and Formula Calculations Easy for Taxpayers to Comply with and for the IRS to Administer?

One concern with the EITC is that its complex rules and formulas make it difficult for taxpayers to comply with and difficult for the Internal Revenue Service (IRS) to administer. Studies indicate that EITC errors by taxpayers (whether intentional or unintentional) result in a relatively high proportion of EITC payments being issued incorrectly. Monitoring for EITC compliance remains a challenge for the IRS.

Taxpayers Challenges Complying with the EITC

Taxpayer error in claiming the EITC has been an ongoing concern with the credit.[72] Evidence suggests that the EITC's complex formulas and eligibility rules may result in taxpayers claiming the EITC in error. For example, a non-custodial parent who pays child support may erroneously assume they can claim that child for the credit—resulting in a larger credit than they would otherwise receive. Hence, taxpayer error—whether intentional or unintentional—can result in significant dollar amounts of the credit being claimed incorrectly.

Taxpayer noncompliance with the EITC is often measured in two ways—improper payments and overclaims.

- EITC overclaims are the amount of the credit claimed incorrectly and do not include the impact of enforcement activities.
- EITC improper payments are an annual fiscal year measure of the amount of the credit that is erroneously claimed (generally overclaimed) net of any amounts recovered by the IRS from their enforcement activities (i.e., audits).73 In other words, recovered amounts of the credit are subtracted from erroneous claims of the credit to calculate improper payments.

Improper payments are generally smaller than overclaims since improper payments net out amounts recovered or protected by the IRS, while overclaims do not. In addition, the amount of EITC improper payments is reported annually. In contrast, overclaims—which are often discussed in research studies of the factors that lead to tax filer noncompliance—have historically been reported less frequently. The last two comprehensive IRS studies that examined overclaims were released in 1999 and 2014.[74]

The IRS estimates that in FY2013, 22% to 26% of EITC payments—between $13.3 billion and $15.6 billion—were issued improperly.[75] EITC improper payments and rates are high when compared to the improper payments and rates of traditional spending programs (discussed further below in "Improper Payments and Administering a Social Benefit Through the Tax Code").[76]

In August 2014, the IRS released its most recent EITC compliance study examining the causes of EITC overclaims on 2006, 2007, and 2008 tax returns (henceforth referred to as the "2006-2008 EITC Compliance Study"). Total overclaims from the 2006-2008 EITC Compliance Study were estimated to be between $14.0 billion and $19.3 billion. The study found that between 79% and 85% of EITC dollars claimed incorrectly were claimed by tax filers ineligible for the credit (as opposed to those eligible for a smaller credit).

This study concluded that there were three major reasons[77] for errors among claimants:

- EITC claimants claimed children who were not their qualifying children for the credit;
- EITC claimants misreported their income; and
- EITC claimants used an incorrect filing status when claiming the credit.

The 2006-2008 EITC Compliance Study found that the *most frequent* EITC error was incorrectly reporting income—in most cases self-employment income—and the largest error (in terms of overclaim dollars) was incorrectly claiming a child for the credit, as illustrated in *Table 6*. The most common qualifying child error was claiming a child who did not fulfill the residency requirement. The study also found that filing status errors are a source of EITC overclaims, although they are a relatively smaller cause of errors in comparison to income reporting and qualifying child errors.

Paid Tax Preparers

Unlike previous studies, the 2006-2008 EITC Compliance Study examined different types of paid tax preparers who prepared tax returns which included EITC claims (these tax returns are sometimes referred to as "EITC returns"). The study found that among paid tax preparers, unenrolled preparers were both the most common type of tax preparers of EITC returns and among the most prone to erroneous claims of the credit. Unenrolled tax preparers generally do not pass the same testing requirements as enrolled preparers (e.g., attorneys and CPAs), and, in contrast to enrolled tax preparers, are limited in how they represent their clients before the IRS. The IRS does not conclude that these data are sufficient to indicate which preparers tend to be less capable or unscrupulous. More research may help to determine "the relative ability or integrity of unenrolled preparers."

Table 6. EITC Overclaims Attributable to Major Types of Error, 2006-2008 Annual Average

			Amount Overclaimed (billions $2008)
Error Type	*Number of Returns with Error (millions)*	*Low Estimate*	*High Estimate*
Income Reporting Error	6.5	$4.5	$5.6
Qualifying Child Error	3.0	$7.2	$10.4
Filing Status Error	1.0	$2.3	$3.3
Total	11.9	$14.0	$19.3
	Addendum		
Total Number of Returns Claiming the EITC	*23.7*	*Total Dollar Amount of EITC Claimed ($2008)*	$49.3

Source: Table 1 (Addendum) and Table 5 of the 2006-2008 EITC Compliance Study.

Note: According to the IRS, the totals may be greater than the sum of each error type due to double counting. First, more than one type of error may occur on a given return. Second the estimate of overclaim dollars treats each error in isolation. Each estimate is calculated assuming the respective error is the only error eliminated. However a given amount of overclaim dollars may occur on a return with multiple errors, with the cost of one error influenced by presence and cost of the other error.

IRS Challenges in Administering the EITC

In addition to taxpayers facing challenges in complying with the EITC rules, the IRS may also face challenges in administering the credit. Specifically, the IRS may or may not be able to detect these errors and administer this tax benefit. Generally, the IRS does not reveal how it detects errors or flags questionable tax returns to prevent persons from using this information to circumvent IRS detection. However, public documents that evaluate the efficacy of the IRS error detection procedures do provide a general overview of *some* of the ways the IRS may attempt to detect errors, especially before a refund is issued. They also indicate challenges the IRS may face in accurately detecting taxpayer error.

One of the largest sources of qualifying child errors is the child failing to meet the EITC's residency requirement. But the IRS does not have a database containing information on children and with whom they live and for how long. While the IRS may use databases like the Federal Case Registry of child support orders (FCR) or various Social Security databases to try to verify the child meets the residency requirement, they may not always be accurate. For example, an IRS study examining the accuracy of the FCR in validating the residency requirement of the EITC found that of a sample of tax returns that FCR data flagged for audit, 23% of these returns once audited were found to have no adjustments in taxes owed. [78] In other words, 23% of these taxpayers were effectively compliant even though the FCR had flagged them as being noncompliant with the residency requirement of the EITC.

Similarly with respect to some income reporting errors, the IRS may not have information to accurately detect errors. Some observers have suggested that to verify income used to claim the credit the IRS may be able to compare income reported on the tax filer's tax return to information reported on third-party forms. In other cases—especially among the self-employed—the IRS may have incomplete information. Self-employed individuals generally have their compensation reported on a Form 1099. But this *compensation* does not necessarily represent self-employment *income*. Taxpayers may deduct a variety of business expenses from their compensation to determine their self-employment income. The IRS, however, does not receive third-party verification of these deductible expenses when a taxpayer files his or her income tax return. In contrast, wage income is directly reported on form W-2 and is provided to both the taxpayer and the IRS. Indeed, the availability of wage income information to both the taxpayer and the IRS may be a factor in the lower dollar amount of overclaims attributable to wage income reporting errors.

While the IRS may have challenges in detecting EITC errors, they are permitted to take certain measures to penalize those taxpayers who claim the credit in error. The IRS can, once they have determined a tax filer improperly claimed the EITC, subject that taxpayer to financial penalties and disallow them from claiming the credit in future years. If upon examination by the IRS, all or part of a taxpayer's EITC is denied, the taxpayer[79]

> (1) must pay back the amount in error with interest; (2) may need to file the Form 8862, Information to Claim Earned Income Credit after Disallowance; (3) may be banned from claiming EITC for the next two years if we [the IRS] find the error is because of reckless or intentional disregard of the rules; or (4) may be banned from claiming EITC for the next ten years if we [the IRS] find the error is because of fraud.

Tax return preparers who erroneously claim the credit on behalf of clients may also be subject to financial penalties, suspension or expulsion from e-file, injunction preventing them from preparing returns or subjecting them to certain limitations, and other disciplinary action.

Improper Payments and Administering a Social Benefit Through the Tax Code

Since the EITC is both a needs-tested transfer to low-income Americans as well as a tax benefit, it is important to put the IRS's challenges in administering the EITC (as well as the high improper payment rate of the credit) in the context of both traditional spending programs and other tax benefits. Often the EITC error rate is compared to the error rates of other spending programs. For example, the Office of Management and Budget (OMB) has designated the EITC as a "high-error program" in comparison to other spending programs, with EITC improper payments the second highest in terms of the total dollar amount (behind Medicare Fee-for-Service) and the highest in terms of improper payment rate (improper payments as a percentage of total payments).[80] However, the EITC is not administered like a traditional spending program, but administered as a tax benefit, which may ultimately affect error rates.

For example, some experts stress that spending programs may have lower improper payment rates than the EITC because they screen *every participant before the benefit can be claimed*. Such screenings generally involve high up-front administrative costs, but may lower the amount of benefits incorrectly paid out. In contrast, the administrative cost of the EITC is relatively minimal. In congressional testimony, the IRS Taxpayer Advocate noted that[81]

> Using tax returns as the "application" for EITC benefits rather than a traditional screening process results in low cost with high participation as well as the risk of improper payment. The IRS has pointed out that for the EITC current administration costs are less than 1% of benefits delivered. This is quite different from other non-tax benefits programs in which administrative costs related to determining eligibility can range as high as 20% of program expenditures.

Minimal pre-filing eligibility verification—generally the norm among tax benefits—may reduce administrative costs but also lead to substantial amounts of the credit being claimed in error.

When revenue losses that arise from EITC errors are compared with other provisions of the tax code, they appear relatively small. A recent IRS report on the tax gap—tax liabilities not paid— found that the largest source of noncompliance with individual income tax laws was the underreporting of business income on individual income tax returns. The IRS estimates that in 2006, the underreporting of business income resulted in reduced revenues of $122 billion.[82] As the Taxpayer Advocate stated in the Fiscal Year 2015 Objectives, when comparing the tax gap from the EITC noncompliance versus underreporting business income, "EITC overclaims account for 6% of the gross individual income tax noncompliance while business income underreported by individuals accounts for 51.9%."[83]

CONCLUDING REMARKS

When initially enacted in the 1970s, there were two major purposes of the EITC. First, the credit was meant to encourage the non-working poor (only those with children) to enter the workforce and be more self-sufficient. Second, the credit was intended to help reduce the tax burdens of working poor families with children. While these families were generally not subject to income taxes, they were subject to payroll taxes on their earnings. Some policymakers at the time worried that payroll taxes would reduce poor families' take home pay to such an extent that they would need to rely on cash welfare. In the 1990s, the purposes of the credit were expanded to include poverty reduction, with a focus on encouraging welfare recipients—generally unmarried mothers—to work.

If policymakers want to modify the EITC, it may be helpful to understand both the benefits and limitations or problems with the credit.[84] Research on the EITC suggests that the EITC has generally achieved many policymakers' original goals: It has encouraged single mothers to enter the workforce and it has reduced poverty among families with children. However, studies also indicate limitations, unintended consequences, or problems with the EITC. Some research suggests it could discourage some married women from working. It has also been shown to exacerbate inequities in the tax code between taxpayers with and without children. In addition, approximately a quarter of all EITC payments are issued improperly. Improper payments are likely related to the complex eligibility rules of the credit, which can be difficult for taxpayers to comply with and difficult for the Internal Revenue Service to verify. For workers without children, the EITC has generally been shown to be ineffective at reducing poverty and no research has indicated it has any effect on encouraging childless individuals to enter the workforce.

APPENDIX. THE ECONOMIC THEORY OF THE IMPACT OF THE EITC ON LABOR SUPPLY

The EITC, in so far as it changes the marginal returns to work (compensation for each hour of work), will theoretically affect both unmarried and married workers' decisions to work and the amount that they work (i.e., the number of hours). The following is a detailed overview of the theoretical impact of the EITC on labor supply decisions (the decision to work and the number of hours worked).

Workforce Participation

According to economic theory, the EITC will unambiguously increase the workforce participation of single workers because these workers can only receive the credit if they work.[85] And those who do not work are no better or worse off as a result of the EITC. As Eissa and Hoynes state "[t]he well-being of a taxpayer who does not work has not changed and any taxpayer who preferred working before [the EITC] will still prefer working, and some taxpayers may find that the additional after-tax income from the EITC makes it worth entering the workforce."[86]

Among married couples however, the theoretical impact the credit has on each spouse's labor force participation may differ and can be understood using the theoretical framework of "income" and "substitution" effects. In summary, when a tax policy, like the EITC, increases the marginal returns to work, this additional income makes the worker feel richer for the same amount of work. If the worker has an income target ("I need to make $200 this week"), an increase in wages from the EITC means they can work *less* to achieve the *same* level of income. Economists refer to this as the "income effect" of the EITC. At the same time, an increase in the marginal return to work means that "not working" or "leisure" implicitly costs more in terms of foregone wages. Hence, the individual will consume less leisure, and work more. This is referred to as the "substitution effect" of the EITC by economists.

Economists generally assume that in a married couple, one spouse is the primary earner, and earns more of the household income than the secondary earner. In addition, economists generally assume that the primary earner makes their labor force participation decision first, and then the secondary earner decides whether to work (this is referred to as sequential family labor supply decisions). In such a model, the primary earner's labor force decision is the same as the one faced by an unmarried worker. They (and their family) will only receive the credit if they work, and hence the labor force participation of primary earners should unambiguously increase.

Given that the value of the EITC for a family is based on the combined earnings of both spouses, the secondary earner's labor force participation decision will depend on the distribution of income between the spouses. If the income of the primary earner is sufficiently low that it places the family in the phase-in region of the credit, then the secondary earner's decision to work will theoretically be ambiguous. On the one hand, by working, the secondary earner would increase the marginal returns to work of the married couple. According to the substitution effect, the secondary earner would be encouraged to work. On the other hand, the family might decide that the additional income from the EITC is sufficient for the family to meet their needs, and according to the income effect, the secondary earner may choose to remain out of the labor force. Given that these two effects move in opposing directions, it is unclear as to whether the labor force participation of secondary earners will increase in this situation, although most empirical research suggests that over this income range, the substitution effect is dominant (and hence the secondary earner will decide to start working).

However, the income of most earners implies that if they were to marry, the combined family income would place the family in the plateau or phase-out range of the credit.[87] Over this income range, the income and substitution effects suggest that the secondary earner would be better off staying out of the labor force, which could lead to a reduction of the labor force participation of these individuals. If the secondary earner were to start working, the family's EITC would either remain constant (if the family remained in the plateau region of the credit), or fall in value (if the family was in the phase-out region of the credit). In either region, the family would still receive a credit, and the income effect would suggest that the secondary earner would be discouraged from entering the workforce. If the family's income placed them in the plateau region, the family would receive the same amount of the EITC regardless of the number of hours worked. In other words, the credit would not increase their hourly wage, and hence would have no substitution effect. If the family's income placed them in the phase-out region of the credit, the value of the credit would fall for each additional hour worked. Hence, the cost of leisure would decline, and according to the substitution effect, a secondary earner would be discouraged from working. Thus, in either case, the combined income and substitution effects would discourage some secondary earners from working.

Hours Worked

Economic theory suggests that the decision workers face in terms of how many hours to work will—like the decision a secondary earner faces in terms of working or not working—depend on the income and substitution effects of the credit. For unmarried workers, the impact of the credit will depend on their individual income, while for married workers the impact will depend on their combined family income. For clarity, the following discussion will refer to a single worker, but the same analysis holds for combined family income of a married couple.

As previously discussed, as the EITC phases in, it increases the marginal return to work for the worker.[88] For example, as illustrated in *Figure 1*, in the phase-in range, one dollar of wages preEITC leads to $1.34 of wages post-EITC. An increase in the marginal return to work, will lead to the worker feeling richer and working less—the income effect—while also simultaneously raising the cost of not working and encouraging workers to work more—the substitution effect. Given these two opposing forces, the theoretical impact of the EITC on hours worked in this earnings range is ambiguous.

For workers whose income places them in the plateau region of the credit, the framework of income and substitution effects implies a worker will work less. In this plateau region, the worker receives the same amount of the EITC no matter how many hours they work. In other words, the credit does not increase their hourly wage, and hence has no substitution effect. But the credit does have an income effect, encouraging that worker to work less. In effect, if workers receive the same credit amount over a range of earnings, economic theory suggests some workers will choose to work the least number of hours to receive the credit (other workers in the plateau region may work more hours to receive more in wages).

As the credit phases out, it decreases a worker's marginal return to work (i.e., in the example in *Figure 1*, every additional dollar of pre-EITC earnings leads to a reduction of the EITC by almost 16 cents). Hence, the cost of leisure declines, and according to the substitution effect, a worker will work fewer hours. Even though the amount of the EITC is falling, it is still greater than zero in this range, meaning it still boosts income. Hence, according to the income effect, a worker will consume more leisure and work less. Therefore, economic theory suggests that workers whose incomes places them in the phase-out region of the credit will work less.

End Notes

[1] The Aid to Families with Dependent Children (AFDC) caseload increased from 0.9 million families (3.4 million recipients) in 1961 to 1.7 million families (6.7 million recipients) in 1969. Congressional Research Service (CRS) compilation of data from the U.S. Department of Health and Human Services (HHS).

[2] In general, a negative income tax would be structured to mirror a positive income tax. In a positive income tax, income above a certain threshold amount (for example, the standard deduction and the appropriate number of personal exemptions), is taxed. In a negative income tax system, the amount of income below a given threshold is refunded to the taxpayer at a given rate. For example, if a threshold was set at $10,000 for an individual, with a tax or refund rate of 10%, a taxpayer with $11,000 of income would pay $10 in tax. A taxpayer with $9,000 in income would receive a $10 refund. Hence, a taxpayer with zero income would receive a $1,000 refund. For more information on negative income tax, see Robert A. Moffitt, "The Negative Income Tax and the Evolution of U.S. Welfare Policy," NBER Working Paper Series | Working Paper 9751, June 2003.

[3] H.R. 16311 in the 91st Congress and H.R. 1 in the 92nd Congress.

[4] V. Joseph Hotz and John Karl Scholz, "The Earned Income Tax Credit," in Means-Tested Transfer Programs in the United States, ed. Robert A. Moffitt, (University of Chicago Press, 2003), p. 142, http://www.nber.org/chapters/ c10256.pdf.

[5] Senator Russell Long, Remarks in the Senate, Congressional Record, September 20, 1972, pp. 33010-33011.

[6] Dennis J. Ventry, "The Collision of Tax and Welfare Politics: The Political History of the Earned Income Tax Credit, 1969-1999," National Tax Journal, vol. 53, no. 4 (December 2000), p. 993.

[7] In addition, "over the years, there were increases in the payroll tax rate, which increased from 2.0% of pay (1.0% each for employees and employers) in the 1937-1949 period to its current level of 12.4%." See CRS Report R42035, Social Security Primer, by Dawn Nuschler.

[8] Senator Russell Long, Remarks in the Senate, Congressional Record, September 20, 1972, p. 33010.

[9] As originally enacted, the credit was equal to 10% of the first $4,000 in earnings. Hence, the maximum credit amount was $400. The credit phased out by 10% between incomes of $4,000 and $8,000.

[10] U.S. Congress, Senate Committee on Finance, Tax Reduction Act of 1975, Report to Accompany H.R. 2166, 94th Cong., 1st sess., March 17, 1975, S. Rept. 94-36, p. 11.

[11] For more information, see "Brief History of Cash Assistance" in CRS Report R43187, Temporary Assistance for Needy Families (TANF): Size and Characteristics of the Cash Assistance Caseload, by Gene Falk.

[12] This law increased the maximum amount of the credit from $400 to $500. Under the 1978 law, the EITC was set at 10% of the first $5,000 of earnings (including net earnings from self-employment). The maximum credit of $500 was received for earnings between $5,000 and $6,000. For each dollar of AGI above $6,000, the EITC was reduced by 12.5 cents, reaching $0 at an AGI of $10,000.

[13] Joint Committee on Taxation, General Explanation of the Revenue Act of 1978, March 12, 1979, JCS-7-79, p. 51.

[14] David Wessel, "Expanded Earned-Income Tax Credit Emerges As the Anti-Poverty Program of Choice for Many," The Wall Street Journal, July 13, 1989, p. A16.

[15] "Presidential Address to Congress," Reuters transcript of a presidential speech as delivered. February 17, 1993.

[16] V. Joseph Hotz and John Karl Scholz, "The Earned Income Tax Credit," in Means-Tested Transfer Programs in the United States, ed. Robert A. Moffitt, (University of Chicago Press, 2003), p. 146, http://www.nber.org/chapters/c10256.pdf.

[17] The distribution of tax burden played an important role in the congressional negotiations of the 1990 Omnibus Reconciliation Act (OBRA90). Indeed, many commentators have noted that the expansion of the amount of the EITC was often discussed "as a straightforward way to alter the distributional characteristics of various deficit-reduction packages" in such a way as to benefit low-income Americans. V. Joseph Hotz and John Karl Scholz, "The Earned Income Tax Credit," in Means-Tested Transfer Programs in the United States, ed. Robert A. Moffitt, (University of Chicago Press, 2003), p. 146, http://www.nber.org/ chapters/c10256.pdf. As part of the 1990 law, beginning in 1991, the credit for the first time was made larger for families with two or more children versus one child. However, these size differences were modest in comparison to what was enacted as part of the Omnibus Reconciliation Act of 1993. For example in 1992, the maximum credit for a tax filer with one child was $1,324. For families with two children the maximum credit was $1,384, $60

more. By contrast, in 1994, the maximum credit for a taxpayer with one child was $2,038, while the maximum credit for a taxpayer with two children was $2,528.

[18] More recently, the American Recovery and Reinvestment Act of 2009 (ARRA; P.L. 111-5) further adjusted the EITC for larger families, enacting on a temporary basis a larger credit for families with three or more children. This change is currently scheduled to expire at the end of 2017.

[19] CRS Issue Brief, Earned Income Tax Credit: Should It Be Increased to End Poverty for the Working Poor, August 10, 1993, by James R. Storey, available upon request.

[20] For a contemporaneous account of the varying approaches to reduce the marriage penalty debated in 2000, see "Senate Panel Approves Marriage Penalty Relief," New York Times, March 31, 2000.

[21] For more information on marriage penalties and bonuses more generally in the tax code, see Joint Committee on Taxation, Overview of Present Law and Economic Analysis Relating to the Marriage Tax Penalty, the Child Tax Credit, and the Alternative Minimum Tax, March 7, 2001, JCX-8-01, pp. 2-6; and CRS Report RL33755, Federal Income Tax Treatment of the Family, by Jane G. Gravelle.

[22] The other major factor that the Joint Committee on Taxation identified as causing a marriage penalty among low income taxpayers was the size of the standard deduction. At the time, the standard deduction for married taxpayers did not equal twice the standard deduction for two singles. See Joint Committee on Taxation, Overview of Present Law and Economic Analysis Relating to the Marriage Tax Penalty, the Child Tax Credit, and the Alternative Minimum Tax, March 7, 2001, JCX-8-01, p. 3.

[23] For a detailed overview of all the eligibility criteria, and a more detailed description of how the credit is calculated, see CRS Report R43805, The Earned Income Tax Credit (EITC): An Overview, by Gene Falk and Margot L. CrandallHollick.

[24] See Figure 10 in CRS Report R43805, The Earned Income Tax Credit (EITC): An Overview, by Gene Falk and Margot L. Crandall-Hollick; and Elaine Maag, "Earned Income Tax Credit in the United States," Journal of Social Security lae, vol. 22, no. 1 (2015), p. 26.

[25] According to Eissa and Hoynes, among less-educated women (generally those with no more than a high school education), "85% of working wives earn less than their husbands." Nada Eissa and Hilary Williamson Hoynes, "Taxes and the Labor Market Participation of Married Couples: The Earned Income Tax Credit," Journal of Public Economics, vol. 88 (2004), p. 1937, http://www9.georgetown.edu/faculty/noe/jpube804.pdf.

[26] As Eissa and Hoynes state, "there is overwhelming evidence that the EITC encourages work among single mothers but little evidence that eligible working women adjust their hours in response to the EITC. Perhaps most striking about these findings is their consistency across different empirical methods ... as well as different EITC expansions." Nada Eissa and Hilary Hoynes, "Behavioral Responses to Taxes: Lessons from the EITC and Labor Supply," NBER Working Paper Series, Working Paper 11729, 2005, p. 11, http://www.nber.org/papers/w11729.pdf.

[27] For example, see Bruce D. Meyer and Da. T. Rosenbaum, "Welfare, the Earned Income Tax Credit, and the Labor Supply of Single Mothers," Quarterly Journal of Economics, vol. 116 (3), August 2001, pp. 1063-1114, http://harrisschool.uchicago.edu/sites/default/files/MeyerRosenbaumQJE01.pdf.

[28] Bruce D. Meyer, "Labor Supply at the Extensive and Intensive Margins: The EITC, Welfare and Hours Worked," American Economic Review, vol. 92, May 2002, pp. 373-379, http://www.ipr.northwestern.edu/publications/docs/workingpapers/2002/IPR-WP-02-04.pdf.

[29] Jeffrey Grogger, "The Effects of Time Limits, the EITC, and Other Policy Changes on Welfare Use, Work, and Income among Female-Head Families," Review of Economics and Statistics, May 2003, p. 405.

[30] National Bureau of Economic Research (NBER), The Earned Income Tax Credit Raises Employment, The NBER Digest, http://www.nber.org/digest/aug06/w11729.html.

[31] Jeffrey Grogger, Welfare Transitions in the 1990s: The Economy, Welfare Policy, and the EITC, National Bureau of Economic Research, January 2003, http://www.nber.org/ papers/ w9472.pdf.

[32] Nada Eissa and Hillary Williamson Hoynes, "Behavioral Responses to Taxes: Lessons from the EITC and Labor Supply," NBER Working Paper Series, Working Paper 11729, 2005, p. 15, http://www.nber.org/papers/w11729.pdf.

[33] David Ellwood, "The Impact of the Earned Income Tax Credit and Social Policy Reforms on Work, Marriage, and Living Arrangements," National Tax Journal, vol. 534 (December), http://www.ntanet.org/NTJ/53/4/ntj-v53n04p1063- 1106-impact-earned-income-tax.pdf. Other research that found a similar negative effect of the EITC on the labor force participation of secondary earners includes Nada Eissa and Hillary Williamson Hoynes, "The Earned Income Tax Credit and the Labor Supply of Married Couples," National Bureau of Economic Research, Working Paper no. 6856, 1998, http://www.nber. org/papers/w6856; and Nada Eissa and Hilary Williamson Hoynes, "Taxes and the Labor Market Participation of Married Couples: The Earned Income Tax Credit," Journal of Public Economics, vol. 88 (2004), p. 1956, http://www9.georgetown.edu/ faculty/noe/jpube804.pdf.

[34] Bradley T. Heim, The Impact of the Earned Income Tax Credit on the Labor Supply of Married Couples: A Structural Estimation, Working Paper: Office of Tax Analysis, U.S. Department of the Treasury, January 12, 2010, p. 22, http://home.comcast. net/~bradheim/files/HeimEITCFamLS.pdf.

[35] Elaine Maag, "Earned Income Tax Credit in the United States," Journal of Social Security Law, vol. 22, no. 1 (2015), p. 26.

[36] For example, if a job would pay an individual $20/hour, the cost to an individual of not working would be $20 per hour of leisure.

[37] In 2008, 71% of head-of-household filers were estimated to have earnings that placed them in the plateau or phaseout range of the EITC. See Tax Policy Center, Table T14-0114 at http://taxpolicycenter.org/numbers/displayatab.cfm? Docid=4171&DocTypeID=7.

[38] Congressional Budget Office, Effective Marginal Tax Rates for Low- and Moderate-Income Workers, November 2012, http://www.cbo.gov/publication/43709, p. 2.

[39] Bruce D. Meyer, "Labor Supply at the Extensive and Intensive Margins: The EITC, Welfare and Hours Worked," American Economic Review, vol. 92, May 2002, pp. 373-379, http://www.ipr.northwestern.edu/publications/docs/ workingpapers/2002/IPR-WP-02-04.pdf.

[40] Congressional Budget Office, Effective Marginal Tax Rates for Low- and Moderate-Income Workers, November 2012, http://www.cbo.gov/publication/43709, p. 2.

[41] Emmanuel Saez, "Do Taxpayers Bunch at Kink Points?" American Economic Journal: Economic Policy, August 2010, p. 181, http://eml.berkeley.edu/~saez/saezAEJ10 bunching.pdf.

[42] Elaine Maag, "Earned Income Tax Credit in the United States," Journal of Social Security Law, vol. 22, no. 1 (2015), p. 25.

[43] Raj Chetty, John N. Friedman, and Emmanuel Saez, "Using Differences in Knowledge Across Neighborhoods to Uncover the Impacts of the EITC on Earnings," NBER Working Paper

Series | Working Paper 18232, July 2012, p. 35, http://eml.berkeley.edu/~saez/chetty-friedman-saezNBER12EITC.pdf.

[44] Ibid, p. 35.

[45] The EITC marriage penalty occurs because (1) the maximum credit for married joint filers is not double the maximum credit for single filers; (2) the income level at which the EITC phases out for married couples is not double the level for singles; and (3) the value of the EITC is affected by the presence and number of children (as well as earnings), and hence marriage may reduce the EITC depending on the number of children each spouse brings to the marriage. The Economic Growth and Tax Relief Reconciliation Act of 2001 (EGTRRA; P.L. 107-16) provided marriage penalty relief for the EITC by raising the phase-out income level of the EITC for married couples by $3,000 in comparison to the phase-out income level for unmarried EITC recipients. The American Recovery and Relief Act of 2009 (ARRA; P.L. 111-5) temporarily increased marriage penalty relief for the EITC by raising the phase-out income level by $5,000 for married couples in 2009 and indexing the $5,000 for tax year 2010. While the American Taxpayer Relief Act of 2012 (ATRA; P.L. 112-240) made the EGTRRA provisions for marriage penalty relief permanent, the increase in marriage penalty relief to $5,000 (indexed for inflation) made by ARRA was extended for only five years (the expansion will sunset on December 31, 2017).

[46] For 2013 levels, see IRS Publication 596, 2013 Earned Income Credit (EIC) Table, http://www.irs.gov/pub/irs-pdf/p596.pdf. The 2014 levels are calculated using the parameters provided in IRS Revenue Procedure 2013-35, http://www.irs.gov/pub/irs-drop/rp-13-35.pdf.

[47] David Ellwood, "The Impact of the Earned Income Tax Credit and Social Policy Reforms on Work, Marriage, and Living Arrangements," National Tax Journal, vol. 53, no. 4 (December 2000), pp. 1063-1106, http://ntj.tax.org/ wwtax%5Cntjrec.nsf/53542C9468D27BA085256AFC007F39D9/$FILE/v53n4p21063.pdf.

[48] Hilary Hoynes, "The EITC Disincentive: A Reply To Paul Trampe," Econ Journal Watch, vol. 4, no. 3 (September 2007), pp. 321-325.

[49] Heim. "The Impact of the Earned Income Tax Credit on the Labor Supply of Married Couples," 22.

[50] The authors do note that "these modest effects, however, mask substantial heterogeneity across the population of married EITC-eligible families. Women in the phase-out range of the credit experience the greatest reductions, between three and 17 percent." See Nada Eissa and Hilary Hoynes, "The Hours of Work Response of Married Couples: Taxes and the Earned Income Tax Credit," April 2004, p. 20, https://gspp.berkeley.edu/assets/uploads/research/pdf/ CESifo_EissaHoynes.pdf.

[51] For more information, see U.S. Department of Labor, Wage and Hour Division. http://www.dol.gov/whd/minimumwage.htm.

[52] CRS Report R41625, Federal Benefits and Services for People with Low Income: Programs, Policy, and Spending, FY2008-FY2009, by Karen Spar.

[53] See Len Burman and Elaine Maag, The War on Poverty Moves to the Tax Code, Tax Policy Center, January 6, 2014, http://www.urban.org/UploadedPDF/1001711-war-on-poverty-moves-to-tax-code.pdf.

[54] For more information, see CRS Report R41999, The Impact of Refundable Tax Credits on Poverty Rates, by Margot L. Crandall-Hollick.

[55] See Table 5a in Kathleen Short, The Research Supplemental Poverty Measure: 2012, U.S. Census Bureau, Current Population Reports, November 2013, http://www.census.gov/prod/2013pubs/p60-247.pdf.

[56] CRS Report R41999, The Impact of Refundable Tax Credits on Poverty Rates, by Margot L. Crandall-Hollick.

[57] In this analysis, the federal poverty level equals the 2014 poverty guidelines provided by the U.S. Department of Health and Human Services. For more information, U.S. Department of Health and Human Services, Office of The Assistant Secretary for Planning and Evaluation, 2014 Poverty Guidelines. http://aspe.hhs.gov/poverty/14poverty.cfm.

[58] For more information, Tax Policy Center, Distribution of Tax Units That Pay No Individual Income Tax; by Expanded Cash Income Level, Current Law, 2014, Table T13-0231, August 29, 2013, http://www.taxpolicycenter.org/ numbers/displayatab.cfm?DocID=3990.

[59] These figures were calculated using the Current Population Survey Table Calculator available at http://www.census.gov/cps/data/cpstablecreator.html. To access this data, under "Data options, "Get Count of: Persons in Poverty Universe (everyone except unrelated individuals under 15)" for the "Latest Year" of "2013" was selected. Under "Define Your Table," the row variables of "family size," "marital status," and "related children under 18," and the column variable of "poverty status-alternative," were selected. Under "Poverty Thresholds," "Official Poverty Thresholds" was selected. And finally, under "Income Definition," the income definition was customized to include all selected sources of income and expenses, except (1) "Economic Recovery Payments," (2) "Public housing and rent subsidies FMR-based estimates," and (3) "Work-related expenses excluding childcare." These figures were compared with ones that were identical, except for under "Income Definition" the federal earned income credit was de-selected as a source of income. The percentage difference in these two poverty rates is reported in Table 3.

[60] There are several reasons why the poorest tax filers (income <$10,000) may, even after including the EITC, still pay on average higher tax rates than the next highest income class of tax filers (income between $10,000 and $20,000). First, this income class may include a greater proportion of recipients of the childless EITC, a relatively small credit compared to EITC recipients with children. Indeed, while over a quarter of tax filers in this income class are eligible for the EITC, they received 4.2% of the total value of the credit in 2013. When examining how the EITC affects only tax filers with children, the poorest tax filers with children do have the lowest average federal tax rate as a result of the EITC. Specifically, the average federal tax rate for those with less than $10,000 of income is -15.4%; among those with income between $10,000 and $20,000, -13.0%; and among those with income between $20,000 and $30,000, -8.0%, increasing as income rises. For more information, see http://www.taxpolicycenter.org/numbers/Content/PDF/T13- 0220.pdf. In addition, the lowest income class in the Tax Policy Center data may also include nonworking populations who are ineligible for the EITC, including retirees and the disabled.

[61] For more information, see Tax Policy Center, The Numbers: Frequently Asked Questions, T07-9999-Tax Model FAQ, August 12, 2008, question #6, http://www.taxpolicycenter.org/ numbers/displayatab.cfm?DocID=1535#q6.

[62] See Julie-Anne Cronin, Portia DeFilippes, and Emily Y. Line, "Effects of Adjusting Distribution Tables for Family Size," National Tax Journal, vol. 65, no. 4 (December 2012), pp. 739-758.

[63] Gravelle and Gravelle use an equivalence scale recommended by the National Academy of Sciences to improve the federal measure of poverty. This equivalence scale adjusts for both family size and the different needs of adults versus children. More information can be found at "Chapter 3: Adjusting Poverty Thresholds," in Measuring Poverty: A New Approach, ed. Constance F. Citro and Robert T. Michael (National Academies Press, 1995), https://www.census.gov/ hhes/povmeas/methodology/nas/report.html.

[64] Jane Gravelle and Jennifer Gravelle, "Horizontal Equity and Family Tax Treatment: The Orphan Child of Tax Policy," National Tax Journal, vol. 59, no. 3 (September 2006).

[65] Using their equivalence scale, Gravelle and Gravelle found that a married couple filing jointly with no children and $10,000 of income was equivalent to a married couple with one child and $12,338 of income, a married couple with two children and $14,498 of income, and a married couple with three children and $16,529 of income. For more information, see Table 1B in Gravelle and Gravelle, "Orphan Tax Policy," 635.

[66] Gravelle and Gravelle, "Orphan Tax Policy," 636.

[67] These equivalence scales are calculated using a three-parameter scale used to calculate equivalent families for the supplemental poverty measure. For one and two adult families, the scale is (adults)^0.5. For single parents the scale is (adults+0.8*first child+0.5*other children)^0.7. For all other families, the scale is (adults+0.5*children)^0.7. For more information see Kathleen Short, The Supplemental Poverty Measure: 2013, U.S. Census Bureau, Current Population Reports, October 2014, p. 19, https://www.census.gov/content/dam/Census/library/publications/2014/demo/p60- 251.pdf.

[68] Gravelle and Gravelle, "Orphan Tax Policy," 636.

[69] The authors also state that the phasing out of the credit as income rises also has an impact on the horizontal inequity of the credit, particularly among married tax filers in comparison to unmarried recipients. Specifically, married tax filers with the same ability to pay as unmarried tax filers need more income, which may result in them being in the phase-out portion of the credit. Hence families with the same "ability to pay" may receive a smaller EITC.

[70] Gravelle and Gravelle, "Orphan Tax Policy," 648.

[71] Gravelle and Gravelle use a formula for an equivalence scale that assumes that there are economies of scale within families, such that a family of four (two children and two adults) needs 235% of the income of a family of one adult. As one assumes greater economies of scale within a family, all else being equal, the horizontal inequity of the tax code increases among "equivalent" low-income tax payers. Conversely, if one assumes that there are no economies of scale, horizontal inequities are lessened—though still exist—among low-income "equivalent" families.

[72] In the mid-1990s, when Congress debated significantly expanding the credit, taxpayer noncompliance was cited as a significant problem. Specifically, many policymakers were concerned by noncompliance rates reported in a Government Accountability Office (GAO) report. This GAO report reported on an IRS study of a sample of EITC returns during a two-week period in January 1994. The "IRS' preliminary analysis of the returns showed that an estimated 29% of the 1.3 million EIC returns filed electronically during the period had claimed too large a refund, and about 13% of the returns filed was estimated by the IRS as having intentionally claimed too much EIC." General Accounting Office, Tax Administration: Earned Income Credit—Data on Noncompliance and Illegal Alien Recipients, GAO/GGD-95-27, October 1994, p. 1. In 2002, the IRS released another study concerning EITC overclaims that also found a significant amount of taxpayer error. See Internal Revenue Service, Compliance Estimates for Earned Income Tax Credit Claimed on 1999 Returns, February 28, 2002, http://www.irs.gov/pub/irs-soi/compeitc.pdf.

[73] The Internal Revenue Service, Compliance Estimates for the Earned Income Tax Credit Claimed on 2006-2008 Returns, Publication 5162, Washington, DC, August 2014, http://www.irs.gov/pub/irs-soi/EITCComplianceStudyTY2006-2008.pdf, p. 2.

[74] For more information on improper payments and overclaims, see CRS Report R43873, The Earned Income Tax Credit (EITC): Administrative and Compliance Challenges, by Margot L. Crandall-Hollick

[75] For more information, see Treasury Inspector General for Tax Administration (TIGTA), The Internal Revenue Service Fiscal Year 2013 Improper Payment Reporting Continues to Not Comply with the Improper Payments Elimination and Recovery Act, March 31, 2014, http://www.treasury.gov/tigta/auditreports/2014reports/ 201440027fr.pdf.

[76] Generally tax provisions are scored as a reduction of revenue. The refundable portion of the EITC however is designated as an outlay, and hence comparable to a spending program. However, noncompliance with other tax laws can result in reduced revenue. The OMB Payment Accuracy does not compare noncompliance in spending programs (improper payments) to noncompliance in tax programs (foregone revenue).

[77] In addition to the major factors identified in the 2006-2008 EITC Compliance Study that lead to EITC overclaims, the study also identified other minor factors that lead to erroneous claims of the credit. These include errors in applying EITC tie-breaker rules when more than one person can claim a qualifying child, not having a valid Social Security number (SSN), not being a U.S. citizen or resident, not being age 25-64 if claiming the childless EITC, and being the dependent of another taxpayer. In the 2006-2008 EITC Compliance Study, approximately 700,000 returns annually included one of these errors, resulting in overclaims of between $900 million to $1.4 billion annually. In comparison, the total number of returns with overclaims is estimated at 11.9 million, resulting in between $14.0 billion and $19.3 billion in overclaims annually.

[78] Internal Revenue Service W&I Research Group 5, Evaluation of Non-Custodial Parents Reported by the Federal Case Registry and their EITC Eligibility, October 2011. This IRS study is not publicly available. A redacted version is available from the author upon request.

[79] See The Internal Revenue Service, EITC Central, Consequences of Not Meeting Your Due Diligence Requirements, October 3, 2014, http://www.eitc.irs.gov/Tax-Preparer-Toolkit/dd/consequences.

[80] For more information, see the U.S. Government's Payment Accuracy website at https://www.paymentaccuracy.gov/ high-priority-programs.

[81] House Committee on Ways and Means, Subcommittee on Oversight, Written Statement of Nina E. Olson, National Taxpayer Advocate, Hearing on Improper Payments in the Administration of Refundable Credits, http://waysandmeans.house.gov/uploadedfiles/ olsen_testimony.pdf, May 25, 2011, p. 9.

[82] The Internal Revenue Service, "Tax Gap for Tax Year 2006," press release, January 6, 2012, http://www.irs.gov/pub/newsroom/overview_tax_gap_2006.pdf.

[83] Taxpayer Advocate Service, Fiscal Year 2015 Objectives Report to Congress: Research Initiatives, Washington, DC, p. 158, http://www.taxpayeradvocate.irs.gov/userfiles/file/ FY15-Full-Report/Research.pdf.

[84] For an overview of legislation introduced in the 113th Congress to modify the EITC, see CRS Report R43763, The Earned Income Tax Credit (EITC): Legislation in the 113th Congress, by Margot L. Crandall-Hollick.

[85] The decision of a worker to go from non-working to working can also be understood using the framework of income and substitution effects. When a worker goes from non-working to working, his or her wage goes from zero to a positive amount. According to the substitution effect, the worker will consume less leisure and hence work more. Crucially, for this worker, there is no income effect from choosing to work, since they have no income to begin with (and conversely already have the maximum amount of leisure). Hence with no

income effect, and a substitution effect resulting in increased work, a non-worker will choose to work.

[86] Nada Eissa and Hilary Williamson Hoynes, "Taxes and the Labor Market Participation of Married Couples: The Earned Income Tax Credit," Journal of Public Economics, vol. 88 (2004), p. 1937, http://www9.georgetown.edu/ faculty/noe/jpube804.pdf.

[87] In 2008, 71% of head-of-household filers were estimated to have earnings that placed them in the plateau or phaseout range of the EITC. See Tax Policy Center, Table T14-0114 at http://taxpolicycenter.org/numbers/displayatab.cfm? Docid=4171&DocTypeID=7.

[88] It is possible that in some cases employers could reduce wages in response to the availability of the EITC. Employer's "recapture" of part of the EITC would lessen the impact the EITC had in increasing the marginal return to work for the worker. However, a variety of factors would limit the extent to which employers could recapture the credit, including both federal and state minimum wages, living wages, and the supply of low-wage workers.

In: The Earned Income Tax Credit
Editor: Judith L. Collins
ISBN: 978-1-63485-632-4

Chapter 3

THE EARNED INCOME TAX CREDIT (EITC): ADMINISTRATIVE AND COMPLIANCE CHALLENGES*

Margot L. Crandall-Hollick

SUMMARY

The Earned Income Tax Credit (EITC) is a refundable tax credit available to eligible workers earning relatively low wages. Since the credit is refundable, an EITC recipient need not owe taxes to receive the benefit. Hence, many low-income workers, especially those with children, can receive significant financial assistance from this tax provision.

Studies indicate that a relatively high proportion of EITC payments are issued incorrectly. The IRS estimates that in FY2013, 22% to 26% of EITC payments—between \$13.3 billion and \$15.6 billion—were issued improperly. These improper payments can be overpayments or underpayments. The IRS's most recent study (released in 2014) of the factors that lead to EITC overclaims—the difference between the amount of EITC claimed by the taxpayer on his or her return and the amount the taxpayer should have claimed—concluded that there were three major reasons that tax filers claimed the wrong amount of the credit:

---

* This is an edited, reformatted and augmented version of a Congressional Research Service publication R43873, prepared for Members and Committees of Congress, dated April 9, 2015.

- *Qualifying child errors:* Some EITC claimants claimed children *who were not qualifying children for the credit*. The most frequent type of qualifying child error was the failure of the tax filer's qualifying child to meet the credit's residency requirement whereby the claimed child must live with the tax filer for over half the year in the United States. This was *the largest error* in terms of dollars of EITC overclaims.
- *Income reporting errors:* Some EITC claimants misreported their incomes. For example, tax filers whose income was above the phase-out threshold amount would receive a larger credit if they underreported their income. This was *the most common* error in terms of its frequency among tax returns which included an EITC claim and also included an overclaim.
- *Filing status errors:* Some EITC claimants used the *incorrect filing status* when claiming the credit. Specifically, married couples were filing as unmarried (as single or head of household) to receive a larger credit.

This IRS study—also referred to as the 2006-2008 EITC Compliance Study in this report, because it examined tax returns between 2006 through 2008—found largely the same results as a previous IRS study on overclaims, released in 1999. The 2014 study also found that the majority of taxpayers who overclaim the EITC are ultimately ineligible for the credit, rather than eligible for a smaller credit. The 2014 study did not estimate the proportion of errors which were intentional (i.e., fraud) versus "honest mistakes" made while attempting to comply with EITC rules.

Unlike previous studies, the 2014 study also examined different types of paid tax preparers who prepared tax returns which included EITC claims (these tax returns are sometimes referred to as "EITC returns"). The study found that among paid tax preparers, unenrolled preparers were both the most common type of tax preparers of EITC returns and among the most prone to erroneous claims of the credit. Unenrolled tax preparers generally do not pass the same testing requirements as enrolled preparers (e.g., attorneys and CPAs) and in contrast to enrolled tax preparers are limited in how they can represent their clients before the IRS.

This report summarizes findings from the 2014 IRS study detailing the factors that can lead to erroneous claims of the credit, and describes the challenges the IRS may face in their efforts to reduce each type of error. It also examines the role of paid tax preparers on EITC error.

INTRODUCTION

The Earned Income Tax Credit (EITC) is a refundable tax credit available to eligible workers earning relatively low wages. Because the credit is refundable, an EITC recipient need not owe taxes to receive the benefit.[1] Hence, many working poor (especially those with children) who have little or no tax liability receive financial assistance from this tax provision. The amount of the EITC is based on a variety of factors, including number of qualifying children, earned income, and tax filing status.

One concern with the EITC is that its complex rules and formulas make it difficult for taxpayers to comply with and difficult for the Internal Revenue Service (IRS) to administer. Studies indicate that EITC errors (both unintentional and intentional) result in a relatively high proportion of EITC payments being issued incorrectly. The IRS's annual report on improper payments estimates that in FY2013, 22% to 26% of EITC payments—between $13.3 billion and $15.6 billion—were issued improperly.[2] Another IRS study (released in 2014) found that the majority of taxpayers who overclaim the EITC are ultimately ineligible for the credit, rather than eligible for a smaller credit. (While the study was released in 2014, it is also referred to as the 2006-2008 EITC Compliance Study in this report, because it examined tax returns between 2006 through 2008.) In addition, the IRS may have difficulty ensuring that tax filers are in compliance with all the parameters of the credit, a problem that may be exacerbated in light of budgetary constraints faced by the agency.

This report summarizes findings from the recently released 2014 IRS study detailing the factors that can lead to erroneous claims of the credit. The report first briefly defines and compares two common measures of EITC noncompliance: improper payments and overclaims. Next, the report provides an overview of the major factors leading to EITC noncompliance identified in the 2014 study on this issue, as well as challenges the IRS may face in their efforts to reduce each type of error. These factors include claiming ineligible children as qualifying children for the credit, income reporting errors, and filing status errors. Finally, the report describes the role of paid preparers in EITC noncompliance.

A Brief Overview of Improper Payments and Overclaims

This report discusses two measures of EITC noncompliance: improper payments and overclaims. Although these two measures of EITC noncompliance are related, they do differ.

- EITC improper payments are an annual fiscal year measure[3] of the amount of the credit that is erroneously claimed (generally overclaimed) and *not recovered* by the IRS. In other words, recovered amounts of the credit are subtracted from erroneous claims of the credit to calculate improper payments.
- EITC overclaims are the amount of the credit claimed incorrectly and *do not include* the impact of enforcement activities.[4]

Why Does the IRS Study Overclaims Instead of Improper Payments in the 2006-2008 EITC Compliance Study?

While the IRS annually reports on improper payments, when they study the reasons why taxpayers make mistakes in claiming the EITC, they look at tax returns with EITC overclaims. Examining returns with overclaims, as opposed to those returns with improper payments, enables the IRS to examine the taxpayer behaviors that lead to erroneous claims of the EITC. If, instead, the IRS studied tax returns with EITC improper payments, their sample would exclude those tax returns whose EITC overclaims were either never paid (due to prerefund compliance checks) or were recovered (as a result of postrefund audits). Excluding these tax returns could result in inaccurate estimates of the major factors that lead to incorrect EITC claims.

Hence, the major difference between improper payments and overclaims is that improper payments net out amounts recovered or protected by the IRS, while overclaims do not. Hence, improper payments are generally smaller than overclaims.

In addition, in contrast to improper payments which are published annually, overclaims have historically been reported less frequently (the last two comprehensive IRS studies that examined overclaims were released in 1999 and 2014). For a more detailed explanation of the relationship between improper payments and overclaims, see the *Appendix*.

IMPROPER PAYMENTS AND ADMINISTRATIVE COSTS OF THE EITC

The IRS estimates that in FY2013, 22% to 26% of EITC payments—between $13.3 billion and $15.6 billion—were issued improperly.[5,6] EITC improper payments and rates are often compared to the improper payments and rates of traditional spending programs. For example, the Office of Management and Budget (OMB) has designated the EITC as a "high-error program" in comparison to other spending programs, with EITC improper payments the second highest in terms of the total dollar amount (behind Medicare Fee-for-Service) and the highest in terms of improper payment rate (improper payments as a percentage of total payments).[7, 8]

However, in order to make accurate comparisons of improper payments between tax benefits and traditional spending programs, it may be necessary to also consider the comparative costs of *administering* tax benefits and spending programs. The federal government must spend money to administer its tax laws—as well as other government benefits (e.g., food stamps, veteran's benefits). The IRS's administrative expenses include processing tax returns, auditing tax returns, and collecting unpaid tax liabilities. To the extent that additional administrative expenses are associated with fewer errors (unintentional mistakes and fraud) and ultimately a reduction in improper payments, these administrative costs should be considered when comparing the improper payments of tax benefits to traditional spending programs.

For example, some experts stress that spending programs may have lower improper payment rates than the EITC because they screen every participant before the benefit can be claimed. Such screenings generally involve high administrative costs. In contrast, the administrative cost of the EITC is relatively minimal. In congressional testimony, the IRS Taxpayer Advocate noted that[9]

> Using tax returns as the "application" for EITC benefits rather than a traditional screening process results in low cost with high participation as well as the risk of improper payment. The IRS has pointed out that for the EITC current administration costs are less than 1% of benefits delivered. This is quite different from other non-tax benefits programs in which administrative costs related to determining eligibility can range as high as 20% of program expenditures.

In addition to comparing the EITC's improper payments to the improper payments of other spending programs, they can also be compared to revenue losses that arise from taxpayer noncompliance with other provisions of the tax code. EITC errors *are not* the major source of revenue losses arising from taxpayer noncompliance. A recent IRS report on the tax gap—tax liabilities not paid—found that there was a $385 billion gap between what tax filers owed and what they paid in 2006.[10] The majority of the tax gap—$296 billion—is associated with the individual income tax. The largest source of noncompliance with individual income tax laws was the underreporting of business income on individual income tax returns. The IRS estimates that in 2006, the underreporting of business income resulted in reduced revenues of $122 billion. As the Taxpayer Advocate stated in the Fiscal Year 2015 Objectives, when comparing the tax gap from the EITC noncompliance versus underreporting business income, "EITC overclaims account for 6% of the gross individual income tax noncompliance while business income underreported by individuals accounts for 51.9%."[11]

TAX FILER ERRORS THAT LEAD TO EITC OVERCLAIMS

In August 2014, the IRS released a new EITC compliance study examining the causes of EITC overclaims on 2006, 2007, and 2008 tax returns (henceforth referred to as the "2006-2008 EITC Compliance Study"). This study found that the majority of tax filers who overclaim the EITC are ineligible for the credit, instead of eligible for a smaller credit. The study found that between 79% and 85% of EITC dollars claimed incorrectly were claimed by tax filers ineligible for the credit.

This study concluded that there were three major reasons[12] for errors among claimants:

- EITC claimants claimed children who were not their qualifying children for the credit;
- EITC claimants misreported their income; and
- EITC claimants used an incorrect filing status when claiming the credit.

The 2006-2008 EITC Compliance Study found that the *most frequent* EITC error was incorrectly reporting income, and the largest error (in terms of overclaim dollars) was incorrectly claiming a child for the credit, as illustrated in *Table 1*. The study also found that filing status errors are a source of EITC overclaims, although they are a relatively smaller cause of errors in comparison to income reporting and qualifying child errors. Unlike previous studies (which did not examine error among paid preparers), this study also found that among paid tax preparers, unenrolled preparers were the most common type of preparers of tax returns which include the EITC. In addition, unenrolled preparers were found to be most prone to error when claiming the credit.

Table 1. EITC Overclaims Attributable to Major Types of Error, 2006-2008 Annual Average

	Amount Overclaimed (billions $2008)		
Error Type	Number of Returns with Error (millions)	Low Estimate	High Estimate
Income Reporting Error	6.5	$4.5	$5.6
Qualifying Child Error	3.0	$7.2	$10.4
Filing Status Error	1.0	$2.3	$3.3
Total	11.9	$14.0	$19.3
	Addendum		
Total Number of Returns Claiming the EITC	23.7	Total Dollar Amount of EITC Claimed ($2008)	$49.3

Source: Table 1 (Addendum) and Table 5 of the 2006-2008 EITC Compliance Study

Note: According to the IRS, the totals may be greater than the sum of each error type due to double counting. First, more than one type of error may occur on a given return. Second the estimate of overclaim dollars treats each error in isolation. Each estimate is calculated assuming the respective error is only error eliminated. However a given amount of overclaim dollars may occur on a return with multiple errors, with the cost of one error influenced by presence and cost of the other error.

Total overclaims from the 2006-2008 EITC Compliance Study were estimated to be between $14.0 billion (low estimate) and $19.3 billion (high estimate).

The 2006-2008 EITC Compliance Study and "High" and "Low" Estimates

The data from the 2006-2008 EITC Compliance Study are a subsample collected from the IRS National Research Program (NRP). The data from each of the three tax years (2006, 2007, and 2008) were representative of the population, but were combined and then averaged to provide a more statistically accurate sample. The NRP selects a representative sample of the tax filing population, and then conducts audits among this sample. Not all taxpayers selected for an audit actually participate and respond to the audit examiner's request for information. The rate of audit nonparticipation is much higher for this subsample (14.6%) than it is for all other taxpayers (2.9%).[13] This can lead to uncertainty when trying to extrapolate results from the sample to the general population. As the IRS states,[14]

> ...when taxpayers do not provide the [audit] examiner with any input, their audit outcomes may not reflect their true circumstance. This is a particular concern for taxpayers claiming the EITC.

To address the uncertainty of the behavior of audit nonparticipants, the 2006-2008 EITC Compliance Study generally provides a range of estimates based on different assumptions. The "high" estimate assumes that *all* audit nonparticipants claimed the credit erroneously. The "low" estimate assumes that noncompliance among audit nonparticipants is approximately at the same level as noncompliance among similar tax filers who do not comply with audits.

Some research suggests that the "low" estimate is the more accurate of the estimates. In her 2014 testimony before Congress, the IRS Taxpayer Advocate Nina Olson notes that based on Taxpayer Advocate Service research "taxpayers who fail to respond to the audit, or who have a late response, may in fact be eligible for the EITC."[15] Hence, the Taxpayer Advocate exclusively uses the "low" estimate.

In other parts of the 2006-2008 EITC Compliance Study, the researchers examine some of the factors that lead to noncompliance among the audit participants exclusively. In this case only one estimate is provided with the disclaimer that it applies to "known errors" (i.e., the portion of the sample population that did participate in the audit).

For policymakers, it may be important to understand not only the types of taxpayer errors that lead to EITC overclaims, but also how the IRS may or may not be able to detect these errors and administer this tax benefit.

The IRS examines a small sample of all tax returns every year, including those with the EITC, to verify that taxpayers are complying with tax laws. In FY2013, the IRS examined over 1.5 million tax returns,[16] of which more than a third (34.6%) included an EITC claim. (By way of comparison, the IRS processed over 240 million returns in the same time period.)[17] The IRS estimated that of $37.1 billion of additional tax owed as a result of all examinations, 6.9% ($2.5 billion) came from tax returns which included an EITC claim.[18]

Generally, the IRS does not reveal how it detects errors or flags questionable tax returns to prevent persons from using this information to circumvent IRS detection. However, public documents that evaluate the efficacy of the IRS error detection procedures do provide a general overview of *some* of the ways the IRS can attempt to detect errors, especially before a refund is issued. An overview and analysis of challenges the IRS may face in detecting and reducing specific errors is provided for each type of error. While not a complete evaluation, they are intended to highlight how the IRS may prevent overclaims from different types of error as well as the agency's limitations in effectively administering the EITC.

In addition to detecting and preventing errors, the IRS can, once they have determined a tax filer improperly claimed the EITC, subject that taxpayer to both financial penalties and disallow them from claiming the credit in future years. If upon examination by the IRS, all or part of a taxpayer's EITC is denied, the taxpayer[19]

> (1) must pay back the amount in error with interest; (2) may need to file the Form 8862, Information to Claim Earned Income Credit after Disallowance; (3) may be banned from claiming EITC for the next two years if we [the IRS] find the error is because of reckless or intentional disregard of the rules; or (4) may be banned from claiming EITC for the next ten years if we [the IRS] find the error is because of fraud.

Tax return preparers who erroneously claim the credit on behalf of clients may also be subject to financial penalties, suspension or expulsion from e-file, injunction preventing them from preparing returns or subjecting them to certain limitations, and other disciplinary action.

Qualifying Child Errors

A child must meet three requirements or "tests" to be considered a "qualifying child" of an EITC claimant. First, the child must have a specific *relationship* to the tax filer (son, daughter, stepchild or foster child, brother, sister, half-brother, half-sister, stepbrother, stepsister, or descendent of such a relative).[20] Second, the child must share a *residence* with the tax filer for more than half the year in the United States.[21] Third, the child must meet certain *age requirements*; namely, the child must be under the age of 19 (or age 24, if a full-time student).[22] These age requirements are waived if the child is permanently and totally disabled. If the child claimed for the EITC does not meet all of these requirements, they are considered to be claimed in error.

Erroneously claiming a child can result in a significant EITC overclaim per taxpayer. For example, in 2014, the maximum credit amount for taxpayers with no qualifying children is $496. This increases to $3,305 for one qualifying child, $5,460 for two qualifying children, and $6,143 for three or more qualifying children.

How Would Expanding the EITC for Childless Workers Affect EITC Overclaims?

Some have proposed expanding the EITC for *childless* workers.

Policymakers may be concerned that increasing the amount of the EITC for childless workers will result in an increase in the dollar amount of erroneous payments. An expansion of the childless EITC, however, will not increase the number or amount of qualifying child errors, since no children are claimed for the credit. Indeed, in some cases it may reduce these errors. For example, a non-custodial parent who erroneously claims the child for the EITC so he can receive a larger credit may instead choose to claim the larger childless EITC.

Childless EITC recipients may still make other errors (relating to income and filing status), that while not as large (in dollar terms) as qualifying child errors, are more common. The expansion of the credit for childless workers may result in these errors becoming more common.

Study Results

The 2006-2008 EITC Compliance Study found that in terms of *dollar amounts* of overclaims, errors in claiming the qualifying child were the largest source of EITC overclaims. Specifically, the 2006-2008 EITC Compliance

Study found that of the aggregate amount overclaimed, 38% of overclaim dollars were associated with a qualifying child error, averaging $2,384 per return in overclaim.[23] (These estimates reflect overclaims from *known errors* where a taxpayer selected for the audit fully participated in the audit. Hence, these numbers are not comparable to the "high" and "low" estimate provided in *Table 1*.) Errors in claiming qualifying children were the second most common error, found on 21% of returns with an EITC overclaim.

Although qualifying children errors were the largest EITC error in dollar terms, the majority of children claimed for the EITC are claimed correctly. The 2006-2008 EITC Compliance Study found that 87% of children were claimed correctly. Of the 13% of children claimed in error, the most frequent type of qualifying child error was the failure of the tax filer's qualifying child to meet the residency requirement.[24] As previously discussed, a qualifying child for the EITC must share a *residence* with the taxpayer for more than half the year in the United States. Taxpayers may claim the EITC in error if they presume that providing for or being a parent of a child entitles them to the EITC. The 2006-2008 EITC Compliance Study found that among those children known to be claimed in error, more than three-quarters (76%) were due to the tax filer's child failing to meet the residency requirement of the credit.[25]

The second most common "qualifying child error," accounting for 20% of known qualifying child errors, was the failure of the child to meet the relationship test. In other words, the child claimed for the EITC *was not* the son, daughter, stepchild, foster child, brother, sister, half-brother, half-sister, stepbrother, or stepsister (or descendent of such a relative) of the EITC claimant.

IRS Enforcement and the Residency Requirement

The failure of taxpayers' children to meet the qualifying child residency requirement is the largest source in dollars of EITC overclaims, and has historically been the largest source of overclaim dollars.

The Taxpayer Advocate in the FY2015 Objectives Report to Congress notes that "the IRS does not focus on EITC errors with the highest level of noncompliance and misses an opportunity to educate taxpayers about the requirements for claiming [the] EITC and preventing future noncompliance."[26] Specifically, the Taxpayer Advocate notes that the IRS tends to disproportionately audit returns associated with children who fail both the residency and relationship test (75% of audited EITC returns for

2012), and audits fewer EITC returns that fail the residency test exclusively (16% of audited EITC returns for 2012). According to the Taxpayer Advocate, "the IRS should focus more of its audit efforts on returns that have qualifying children with only residency issues, instead of primarily focusing on returns with qualifying children having both relationship and residency issues."[27]

The Taxpayer Advocate also noted that the database and selection criteria used to screen EITC returns for audit during tax filing season failed to detect most noncompliant taxpayers that participated in the 2006-2008 EITC Compliance Study and erroneously claimed a child for the EITC.

Challenges in Detecting and Reducing the Error

When the IRS receives a federal income tax return from a taxpayer with qualifying children claiming the EITC, it may have limited data to verify that the child meets the relevant EITC requirements. As previously discussed, one of the largest sources of qualifying child errors is the child failing to meet the EITC's residency requirement. Currently the IRS may have the authority to use the Federal Case Registry of child support orders (FCR) to attempt to determine if the child is living with the EITC claimant during the filing season, and summarily deny the credit if a claimant is deemed ineligible.[28] Summarily denying the credit effectively means that the refund money is "stopped before going out the door," as opposed to issuing the refund and then verifying information after filing season. Researchers have suggested using the FCR data because

> ...the case registry identifies child support payees and child support payors. It [is] further assumed that the payee generally has physical custody of the child. If the assumption is true, then EITC claims made by someone other than the child support payee would be noncompliant since they would not meet the "residence test" that requires an EITC qualifying child to live with the claimant for more than half the year.[29]

However, the IRS does not currently use the FCR during filing season to summarily deny claims[30] (although they may use it after the filing season is concluded in audits of tax returns including the EITC). Indeed, in response to the Treasury Inspector General recommendation to use the FCR during filing season to summarily deny the credit, the IRS has stated that it will "conduct a study" to determine the accuracy of this database for administration of the EITC.[31]

The IRS may be concerned with the accuracy of using the FCR data to deny the credit during the filing season, without first requesting additional information from the claimant. For example, a court order may require that the custodial parent of the child be the mother. Hence, the father would be the noncustodial parent, and based on the FCR, the father would be ineligible to claim the child for the credit. However, if due to some unforeseen circumstances, like the mother's job loss, the child moved in with the father for a given year, without notifying the court, this change *would not* be noted in the FCR. The child would now (assuming the child met the age test) be the qualifying child of the father for the purposes of claiming the EITC. However, based on the FCR data alone, the father would be incorrectly denied the EITC. As the Taxpayer Advocate has stated with respect to using the FCR to summarily deny the EITC during filing season,[32]

> ...applying data collected for other purposes to an EITC claim is akin to verifying addresses with a telephone directory to deny a home mortgage interest deduction. Even if virtually all of the entries in a directory were accurate, they were compiled for a different purpose, do not disprove eligibility under the tax law, were compiled at a prior date and many not be current, and should not deprive a taxpayer of a due process right to present his or her own facts.

To verify a child meets the residency requirement of the EITC, the IRS has several Social Security Administration databases to verify the relationship test. These include DM-1, which contains the names, Social Security numbers (SSNs), and dates of birth for all SSN holders; Kidlink, which links SSNs of children to at least one of their parents (but only for children who received SSNs after 1998); and Numident, which provides information from birth certificates, including parents' names.[33] Currently, it appears that the IRS does not cross-reference *all EITC* returns to these databases during the filing season. This may be due to limitations of these databases to accurately document that the child fulfills the relationship requirement. As the IRS Taxpayer Advocate has stated, "a child's relationship and residence with respect to a low-income taxpayer are highly circumstantial facts to be validated on a case-by-case basis."[34,35]

Instead, in conjunction with the Federal Case Registry, the IRS may use these databases to construct filters that identify EITC returns with a high probability of error in claiming a qualifying child for the credit. After a return is flagged "the return is placed in queue for possible prefund or post-refund audit. Depending on available resources, [the] IRS will audit a portion of the returns ... before complete refunds are sent to the taxpayers. To the extent returns are not handled in prerefund audits, [the] IRS will include them for possible postrefund audits."[36] Nonetheless, it is generally harder to recover refunds that have already been released as opposed to those denied during filing season.

Income Reporting Errors

The amount of the EITC depends in part on a taxpayer's income. For a taxpayer with a given number of children and marital status, the EITC is structured to vary by income—gradually increasing, then remaining constant at its maximum level, and finally gradually declining in value. *Figure 1* illustrates the EITC amount by earnings level for an unmarried taxpayer with one child for 2014. It illustrates the three distinct ranges of EITC's value by income, with specific dollar amounts and rates applicable to this type of family:

- *Phase-in Range:* The EITC increases with earnings from the first dollar of earnings up to earnings of $9,720. Over this earnings range, the credit equals the *credit rate* (34% for a tax filer with one child) times the amount of annual earnings. The $9,720 threshold is called the *earned income amount* and is the earnings level at which the EITC ceases to increase with earned income. The income interval up to the earned income amount, where the EITC increases with earnings, is known as the phase-in range.
- *Plateau:* The EITC remains at its maximum level of $3,305 from the earned income amount ($9,720) until earnings exceed $17,830. The $3,305 credit represents the *maximum credit* for a tax filer with one child in 2014. The income interval over which the EITC remains at its maximum value is often referred to as the plateau.
- *Phase-out Range:* Once earnings (or adjusted gross income (AGI), whichever is greater) exceed $17,830, the EITC is reduced for every additional dollar over that amount. The $17,830 threshold is known as the *phase-out amount threshold* for a single taxpayer with one child in 2014. For each dollar over the phase-out amount threshold, the EITC is reduced by 15.98%. The 15.98% rate is known as the *phase-out*

rate. The income interval from the phase-out income level until the EITC is completely phased out is known as the *phase-out range*.

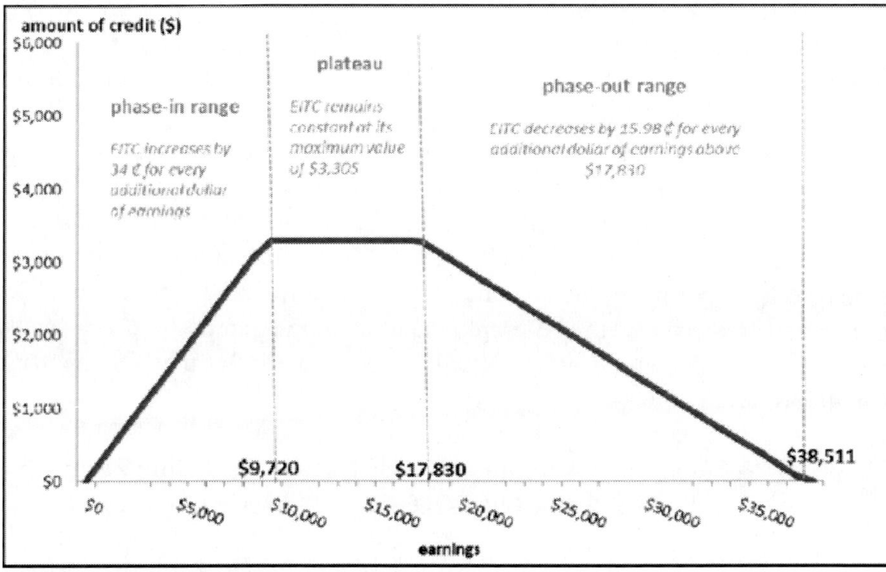

Source: Congressional Research Service.

Figure 1. Amount of the EITC for an Unmarried Tax Filer with One Qualifying Child, 2014.

Incorrectly reporting income (sometimes referred to as "income misreporting") was the most common source of error identified in the 2006-2008 EITC Compliance Study.[37] Income can be overreported or underreported to increase the value of the credit. For tax filers with earnings below the earned income amount, overreporting income can result in a larger credit.[38] In contrast, tax filers whose income is above the phase-out threshold amount may receive a larger credit if they underreport their income. Income underreporting may be more common than overreporting since the majority of EITC claimants—51.8% of claimants in 2008—have income that places them in the phase-out range of the credit.[39]

Study Results

The 2006-2008 EITC Compliance Study found that errors in income reporting were the second-largest source of EITC overclaims, in terms of *dollar amounts* of overclaims. Specifically, the 2006-2008 EITC Compliance Study found that of the total dollar amount overclaimed, 35% was associated with income reporting errors, averaging $807 per return in overclaimed credit.[40] (These estimates reflect overclaims from *known errors* where a taxpayer selected for the audit fully participated in the audit. Hence, these numbers are not comparable to the "high" and "low" estimates provided in *Table 1*). In terms *of number of returns* with an EITC overclaim, known errors related to incorrectly reporting income were the most common error and found on 58% of returns with an EITC overclaim.[41]

As illustrated in *Table 2*, the most frequent type of income reporting error in the 2006-2008 EITC Compliance Study was incorrectly reporting earned income, primarily self-employment income. According to estimates based on audit results, $3.7 billion to $4.5 billion in EITC overclaims were attributable to incorrectly reporting earned income, of which between $3.2 billion and $3.8 billion was associated with self-employment income misreporting. Incorrectly reporting wage income was the smallest contributor to income reporting overclaims.

Table 2. Frequency and Amount of Major Income Reporting Errors by Type of Error (2006-2008 annual average)

	Number of Returns with Error	Total Overclaimed Dollars (billions $2008)	
Types of Income Reporting Error	(millions)[a]	Low Estimate	High estimate
All Income Reporting Errors	6.5	$4.5	$5.6
Earned Income Reporting Errors	4.5	$3.7	$4.5
Wage Income	1.7	$0.8	$1.1
Self-Employment Income	3.1	$3.2	$3.8
AGIb, Investment Income Reporting errors	3.1	$1.1	$1.5

Source: Table 5 of the 2006-2008 EITC Compliance Study, http://www.irs.gov/pub/ irs-soi/ EITCComplianceStudyTY2006-2008.pdf.

Notes: According to the IRS, the values for all income reporting errors are not equal to the sum of the different types of income reporting errors since more than one type of error may occur on a tax return. Estimates of the dollar amounts of overclaims by error type are calculated assuming a particular error type is the only error eliminated.

[a] These estimates are the "high estimate." A low estimate for each error type is not available.

[b] Adjusted gross income, AGI, is equal to total income net of total above-the-line deductions. For purposes of the phase-out of the EITC only, taxpayers must use earned income or AGI, whichever is greater, to determine the value of the credit.

The major sources of income reporting errors are different from the major sources of income among EITC claimants. Most EITC recipients—76%—only have wage income. In contrast, 24% earn at least some self-employment income and 10% report both wages and self-employment income.[42] Hence, the majority of income reporting errors come from a minority of taxpayers, namely those with self-employment income.

Challenges in Detecting and Reducing the Error

In the administration of the EITC, some observers have suggested that the IRS may be able to compare income reported on the tax filer's tax return to information reported on third-party forms. In other cases—especially among the self-employed—the IRS may have incomplete information. Self-employed individuals generally have their compensation reported on a Form 1099. But this *compensation* does not necessarily represent self-employment *income*. Taxpayers may deduct a variety of business expenses from their compensation to determine their self-employment income. The IRS, however, does not receive third-party verification of these deductible expenses when a taxpayer files his or her income tax return. In contrast, wage income is directly reported on form W-2 and is provided to both the taxpayer and the IRS. Indeed, the availability of wage income information to both the taxpayer and the IRS may be a factor in the lower dollar amount of overclaims attributable to wage income reporting errors.

Another factor that may result in income reporting errors is that the IRS receives third-party reporting data on income from employers several months after returns are processed. As previously discussed, wage income is reported on the Form W-2 (and other forms of compensation are reported on other forms like the 1099-MISC). However, "it takes several months for the IRS to process and compile the third-party information."[43] A recent GAO study found that in 2012, for example, the "IRS issued 50% of tax year 2011 refunds to individuals by the end of February, but had only received 3% of information returns."[44] Without timely income information, the IRS may find it difficult to prevent overclaims associated with income reporting errors.

Filing Status Errors

The EITC can be claimed by taxpayers filing their tax return as married filing jointly, head of household, or single. Tax filers cannot claim the EITC if they use the filing status of married filing separately.

The EITC's value depends in part on the tax filer's filing status. Notably, as a result of the structure of the EITC, certain married tax filers may receive a smaller EITC as a married couple than the combined EITC they would receive as two unmarried individuals—often referred to as the EITC "marriage penalty." For example, in 2014, two single parents, each with one child and earned income of $15,000, would receive an EITC of $3,305 each for a total EITC of $6,610. If they married, their combined income would be $30,000, and with two children their EITC would be $4,041.[45] The EITC marriage penalty for this couple would be $2,659. (While some EITC claimants are subject to a marriage penalty, and hence may have an incentive to claim the credit as unmarried, other tax filers may be subject to an EITC marriage bonus. These recipients receive a larger credit as a married couple than their combined credit as two singles.)[46] The IRS states that most EITC filing status errors arise as a result of a married couple filing two separate returns as unmarried tax filers. In other words, most filing status errors likely occur among married tax filers subject to a marriage penalty and who incorrectly file as "head of household" or "single," when they should file as married filing jointly.

Study Results

The 2006-2008 EITC Compliance Study found that filing status errors were the third-largest EITC error in dollar terms, accounting for between $2.3 billion and $3.3 billion of EITC overclaims, illustrated in *Table 1*. According to the study results, filing status errors fall "somewhere between self-employment income misreporting and other types of income misreporting in relative importance."[47] In many cases where the wrong filing status was used, "using the proper filing status would have substantially reduced the amount of the EITC received or made those taxpayers ineligible for the credit altogether."[48] Unlike qualifying child and income reporting errors, a more detailed evaluation of this EITC error was not provided by the IRS in this study.

Challenges in Detecting and Reducing the Error

When taxpayers file their income tax returns, they must select the appropriate filing status based on their marital status and the presence of dependent children. The IRS does not request third-party documentation to verify a taxpayer's marital status during filing season. Indeed, such a request could be viewed as intrusive and burdensome. Instead, the IRS may use marital data from the Social Security Administration to flag questionable returns. There is currently a lack of public information on how the IRS may detect filing status errors.

Paid Tax Preparer Errors

EITC Errors: Fraud or an Honest Mistake?

IRS studies on factors leading to improper payments or overclaims of the EITC generally do not differentiate between intentional errors—fraud—versus unintentional mistakes. For example, if a non-custodial parent claimed a child for the EITC, it is unclear whether they did so intentionally to get a bigger credit or whether they simply assumed they were eligible for the credit because they claimed other child-related tax benefits for the same child. Research from the 1990s suggests that unintentional errors may be the majority of errors in the EITC, as errors in claiming children for example "are correlated with low levels of education, income, and wealth, perhaps because less-educated taxpayers are more likely to make unintentional errors."[49] Another study found that for every 24 cents of improper EITC payments that went to ineligible taxpayers, 11 cents went to taxpayers fraudulently claiming a qualifying child and 13 cents went to those making inadvertent errors.[50]

Until it is known to what extent EITC errors are intentional versus unintentional, it is difficult to determine the most appropriate policy response. Insofar as errors are due to fraud, increasing enforcement activities and auditing could be an appropriate response. However, insofar as errors are due to "honest mistakes," it could be beneficial to simplify some of the rules related to the EITC. It also may be useful to increase educational outreach, since tax filers tend to cycle in and out of the EITC. Recent estimates suggest that a third of tax filers who claim the EITC in a given year have not claimed the credit the previous year.[51] They may be unfamiliar with the eligibility rules and may claim the credit based on incorrect information.

A large number of tax returns are completed by paid tax preparers, especially those who are not regulated by the IRS. (Generally, attorneys, CPAs, and enrolled agents are regulated by the IRS.) For tax year 2011, taxpayers filed about 142 million 1040-series individual returns, with nearly 79 million taxpayers using paid preparers. More than half (over 42 million) of these returns were prepared by preparers who are currently unregulated by the IRS.[52]

Historically, a majority of EITC claimants—approximately two-thirds—have used a paid tax preparer.[53] EITC recipients may use paid preparers for a number of reasons, including the following:

- the belief that having their tax return prepared by a paid preparer will result in a larger tax refund and fewer errors,
- the belief that refunds are received faster when the return is prepared by a paid preparer,
- language differences or taxpayer literacy problems,
- the IRS's close review of EITC returns or the belief that using a paid preparer will reduce the chance of audit,
- less effort (work) by the tax filer, and
- the incorrect belief that the paid preparer (and not the taxpayer) will pay any penalty associated with an error.

However, use of a paid tax preparer does not guarantee an accurate tax return as tax preparers vary in terms of training and experience.

Study Results

The 2006-2008 EITC Compliance Study collected data on both the usage of different types of paid preparers among EITC claimants, and overclaims among these different types of preparers, as illustrated in *Table 3*. The data indicate that among those who reported using a paid preparer, EITC claimants were more likely to use an unenrolled agent[54] or tax preparer from a national tax preparation company (43% and 35%, respectively) compared to non-EITC claimants (28% and 14%, respectively). Notably, unenrolled preparers have a higher frequency of overclaims (between 49% and 54% of EITC returns prepared by these preparers had an overclaim) than almost all other types of paid preparers, including attorneys (35%), CPAs (between 47% and 49%), and enrolled agents (between 42% and 46%). Volunteer tax preparation services provided by the IRS had the lowest frequency of overclaims (between 20% and 26% of EITC returns prepared by IRS volunteer programs had an overclaim).

EITC returns prepared by unenrolled agents also account for the highest percentage of overclaim dollars (the ratio of total overclaim dollars to total claim dollars, by preparer). The IRS estimates that of the $14.5 billion of EITC claimed on tax returns prepared by unenrolled agents, between $4.7 billion and $5.8 billion (33% to 40%) was overclaimed. In comparison, the IRS estimates that between $2.4 billion and $3.6 billion (20% to 30%) of the $11.8 billion of EITC claimed on tax returns prepared by national tax return preparation firms was overclaimed. Tax returns prepared by IRS volunteer services processed $0.8 billion of EITC claims, of which between 11% and 13% was overclaimed.

Table 3. Tax Preparers Used by EITC Claimants and Percentage of Prepared Returns with Overclaims, by Type of Preparer (2006-2008 Annual Average)

	Returns w/o EITC				Returns w/ EITC		
Type of Preparer	% of All Returns	% of Returns Using a Known Paid Preparer[a]	% of All Returns	% of Returns Using a Known Paid Preparer[a]	% of Returns w/Over-claims (low-high estimate)	Dollar Overclaims as % of Total Claims (low-high estimate)	Total Claims (Billions of Constant 2008 $)
Self-Prepared[b]	43%	—	29%	—	39%-47%	28%-39%	$12.0
IRS VITA/TCE[c]	2%	—	3%	—	20%-26%	11%-13%	$0.8
Paid Preparer	55%	—	68%	—	44%-51%	29%-39%	$36.4
Attorney	1%	2%	0%	0%	35%-35%	28%-28%	$0.1
CPA	16%	44%	6%	10%	47%-49%	27%-31%	$2.6
Enrolled Agent	4%	11%	6%	9%	42%-46%	24%-29%	$2.8
Paid Friend/Relative	1%	2%	1%	2%	37%-37%	19%-19%	$0.5
National Tax Return Prep Firm	5%	14%	21%	35%	35%-44%	20%-30%	$11.8
Unenrolled Return Preparer	10%	28%	26%	43%	49%-54%	33%-40%	$14.5
Preparer Used, Type Unknown[d]	18%	—	8%	—	51%-72%	47%-73%	$4.1
TOTAL	100%	100%	100%	100%	42%-49%	29%-38%	$49.1

Source: The Internal Revenue Service, Compliance Estimates for the Earned Income Tax Credit Claimed on 2006- 2008 Returns, Publication 5162, Washington, DC, August 2014, Tables 8 and 9.

[a] These percentages are based on data from taxpayers who reported using a particular type of paid preparer.

[b] Self-prepared returns include those where the taxpayer reported receiving uncompensated assistance from another individual. For self-preparers claiming the

EITYV, 28% received this assistance among those not claiming the EITC, 9% received informal assistance.

[c] The majority of the returns in this category were prepared by the Volunteer Income Tax Assistance (VITA) program or Tax Counseling for the Elderly (TCE). Approximately 3% were prepared by the IRS via other venues.

[d] The majority of the returns in the category were cases where the return was accepted as filed with no investigation into the type of preparer used. A large number of audit non-participants are also included in this group.

The IRS does not conclude that these data are sufficient to indicate which preparers tend to be less capable or unscrupulous. A 2008 Taxpayer Advocate study found that both taxpayers and tax preparers tend to fall into one of three groups: (1) those intent to commit fraud and understate their liabilities or overstate their refunds; (2) those who are indifferent and who defer decisions to the other party (i.e., the tax preparer defers to the taxpayer and vice versa); and (3) those who seek to comply with the tax laws. As this study stated, it is important to understand the dynamic relationship between taxpayers and paid preparers. Certain compliant paid preparers might choose not to assist people who seek to claim the EITC incorrectly. Conversely, a noncompliant taxpayer may seek out a noncompliant paid preparer.[55] Echoing this idea, the IRS in the 2006-2008 EITC Compliance Study notes that error rates among preparers may be influenced by selection bias. For example, taxpayers with more complicated tax returns, or who are seeking to intentionally overclaim the credit, may seek out an unenrolled agent. More research may help to determine "the relative ability or integrity of unenrolled preparers."[56]

Several Government Accountability Office (GAO) investigations of small samples of returns prepared by paid tax preparers have also highlighted the variability in quality and accuracy of paid tax preparation services. In a 2014 study, GAO found that of their limited sample of paid tax preparers (19), most of them (17) made some mistakes when preparing tax returns that resulted in an incorrect refund amount.[57] As GAO reported, "nearly all of the returns prepared for our undercover investigations were incorrect to some degrees, and several of the preparers gave us incorrect advice, particularly when it came to reporting non-Form W-2 income (i.e., wage income) and the EITC. Only 2 of the 19 tax returns showed the correct refund amount."[58] The report also found that in 3 out of 10 cases, the tax preparers claimed an ineligible child for the EITC.[59] In other cases, the tax preparers did not report cash tips of the taxpayer, leading to overstated refunds. Overstated refunds resulting from these two errors ranged from $654 (underreporting income) to $3,718 (underreporting income and claiming an ineligible child).

Challenges in Detecting and Reducing the Error

There have been a variety of proposals to improve the quality of services by paid tax preparers and to increase compliance among these preparers. Under current law, since 2011 paid tax preparers who prepare returns which include an EITC claim must follow several due diligence requirements, including the following:

- Completing IRS Form 8867 and filing this form with each tax return they prepare. Form 8867 is a checklist for the preparers asking questions concerning the taxpayer's filing status, income, and any children claimed for the credit.[60]
- Completing an EITC worksheet found in the Form 1040 instructional booklet.
- "Tak[ing] steps to ensure that all taxpayer information provided to them is correct and complete by asking follow-up questions to the taxpayer and requesting additional documentation."[61]

Copies of all forms and relevant information must be kept by the preparer for three years. Paid preparers who do not meet these requirements can face a penalty of up to $500 for each return for which they fail to meet the due diligence requirements.

In addition, the IRS requires that any individual who prepares a tax return for compensation must obtain a Preparer Taxpayer Identification Number (PTIN).[62] A PTIN is intended to enable the IRS to quickly and efficiently identify tax preparers who prepare tax returns with a high number of errors or overclaims. Some advocates, however, have pushed for more regulation at the federal level of paid preparers.[63] Before January 2013, the IRS had also begun implementation of new testing and continuing education requirements for certain paid preparers not already subject to IRS oversight.[64] A Treasury Inspector General Report on EITC improper payments noted that these initiatives to regulate previously unregulated preparers were "considered the most promising strategy for curbing EITC improper payments."[65] However, as a result of a ruling in *Loving v. Internal Revenue Service* in 2013, the IRS was enjoined from enforcing these new requirements.[66] Ultimately, the IRS chose not to appeal the decision in *Loving.*[67] The IRS has stated that it may consider a voluntary education and testing program for unregulated preparers.[68]

Congress has in the past introduced legislation that would give the IRS the statutory authority to regulate paid tax preparers, including S. 832 in the 109th Congress and S. 1219 in the 110th Congress. More recently, the Senate Finance committee held a hearing in 2014 concerning paid preparers. At that hearing the IRS Commissioner requested Congress provide the IRS with the explicit legal authority to regulate currently unregulated tax preparers.[69] In the 113th Congress, no legislation was introduced to regulate paid tax preparers.

Concluding Remarks

In summary, the recent EITC compliance study found that the most common error tax filers make when claiming the EITC is incorrectly reporting income. The largest EITC error in dollar terms is incorrectly claiming a child for the credit. The 2006-2008 EITC Compliance Study however, did not provide estimates of what proportion of EITC errors were due to taxpayer confusion versus intentional error (i.e., fraud). This may be of particular interest to policymakers seeking to reduce EITC errors because the strategies to reduce "honest mistakes" versus "fraud" differ. Insofar as these errors are due to taxpayer (or paid tax preparer) confusion with the EITC eligibility rules, the most effective policy response may be to simplify these rules and create greater uniformity for all child-related tax benefits in conjunction with increasing taxpayer education on EITC eligibility. This may be particularly relevant for EITC claimants given that about one-third of the EITC claimants in a given year did not participate in the program the previous year[70] and may be unfamiliar with the complex eligibility requirements of the credit.

Increasing enforcement activities and auditing could be the best policy response for errors resulting from fraudulent claims of the credit. The IRS would need data on taxpayers' compliance with EITC parameters (e.g., whether the child claimed was a qualifying child) to enforce the rules of the credit. However, the IRS currently may not have sufficient information to verify qualifying child eligibility and self-employment income. The issues surrounding the IRS ability to detect and correct EITC errors highlight a more general problem with administering complex provisions like the EITC—the lack of accurate and timely third-party data to verify complex eligibility rules. The IRS's budgetary constraints may also hinder enforcement activities. Problems with administration of the EITC also highlight more general problems of administering a variety of child-related tax benefits (like the dependent exemption, the child tax credit, and the child and dependent care credit), each with slightly different eligibility rules. A taxpayer, for example, may incorrectly believe that eligibility for one child-related tax benefit, like the child tax credit, makes them eligible for the EITC, and vice versa, when that may not be the case.

There are a variety of legislative options to improve the administration of the EITC, alone and in the context of other child-related tax benefits. Congress could simplify tax provisions such that they are enforceable with current third-party data (e.g., by making the EITC purely a work-based credit, based on earnings, not qualifying children). Or Congress could simplify eligibility for all child-related tax benefits, such that a qualifying child for one benefit would be a qualifying child for all other child-related tax benefits.

The IRS's administration of the EITC has highlighted the agency's shifting role from tax collector to tax collector *and* benefit administrator. Unlike other agencies that administer social and economic benefit programs, the IRS does not expend significant resources to determine a taxpayer's eligibility for the EITC *before* a tax return is filed. Instead, taxpayers file for the EITC, and then the IRS may verify if the taxpayer is eligible for the credit. Some tax returns are checked during tax filing season and others are checked post filing season, after the credit has been paid. Minimal pre-filing eligibility verification may reduce administrative costs but also lead to substantial amounts of the credit being claimed in error.

More broadly, improper payments of refundable tax credits may increase as the number of refundable credits the IRS administers increases or participation in existing credits increases. Given the high percentage of EITC improper payments and data limitations in detecting certain EITC errors, Congress may choose to reconsider providing social benefits through the tax code in the form of refundable credits. Alternatively, if Congress remained interested in providing social benefits in the form of refundable tax credits, the IRS's mission statement could be broadened to include both tax collection *and* the administration of social benefits.[71] Without any changes in the way the IRS administers social benefits like the EITC, improper payments of refundable credits and the suitability of the IRS in administering social benefits could continue to be a prominent issue in tax administration.[72]

Appendix. The Relationship Between Improper Payments and Overclaims

As previously mentioned, this report discusses two measures of EITC noncompliance: improper payments and overclaims. Although these two measures of EITC noncompliance are related, they do differ.

Improper payments are an annual fiscal year measure[73] of the amount of the credit that is erroneously claimed and *not recovered* by the IRS. Overclaims and the overclaim rate are the amount of the credit claimed incorrectly on successfully processed tax returns and *do not include* the impact of enforcement activities.[74] In addition, overclaims and the overclaim rate are generally reported less frequently than improper payments and the improper payment rate. The IRS released studies in 1999 and 2014 which examined EITC overclaims.

Improper Payments, the Improper Payment Rate, and Overclaims

EITC improper payments are defined as erroneous amounts of the credit (including both the nonrefundable and refundable portion of the credit) that are "paid out to taxpayers and are not later recovered or corrected by the IRS."[75] To determine an estimate of the *dollar amount of improper payments* in a given fiscal year, an estimated *improper payment rate* is multiplied by an estimate of *total EITC claims* for that fiscal year.

The estimated improper payment rate is based on a sample of the most recent individual income tax reporting compliance data, which can be several years older than the estimate of total EITC claims. For example, the estimated improper payment rate used to estimate the dollar amount of improper payments in FY2012 used tax data from 2008 tax returns. This estimated improper payment rate (based on a sample of 2008 tax returns) was then multiplied by an estimate of total EITC claims for FY2012 to determine the dollar amount of improper payments for FY2012.

An EITC overclaim is "the difference between the EITC amount claimed by the taxpayer on his or her return and the amount the taxpayer *should* have claimed."[76] To determine why some tax filers erroneously claim the EITC, the IRS examines tax returns with an EITC overclaim instead of examining returns with an improper payment. This allows the IRS to determine the factors that lead tax filers to claim the credit incorrectly. If instead, the IRS examined tax returns with EITC improper payments, their sample would exclude those tax returns whose EITC overclaims were either never paid (due to prerefund compliance checks) or were recovered (as a result of postrefund audits). Excluding these tax returns could result in inaccurate estimates of the major factors that lead to incorrect EITC claims.

Before FY2013, the EITC improper payment rate was calculated as total overclaims dollars net of EITC overclaim dollars recovered, divided by the total amount of EITC dollars claimed on all returns. Beginning in FY2013,[77] the IRS's calculation of improper payments includes underpayments. EITC underpayments are "the amount of the EITC disallowed by the IRS in processing that *should have* been allowed."[78] Under this new calculation of the improper payment rate, the dollar amounts of underpayments and overclaims are *added together* and the total amount of recovered EITC overclaims is then subtracted from this sum (see *Figure A-1*). This modification has a small effect on the improper payment rate, with Treasury noting that "underpayments increase the overall improper payment rate by less than 0.05 percent."[79]

$$\text{Improper Payment Rate} = \frac{\text{Overclaims} + \text{Underpayments} - \text{Claims Protected or Recovered}}{\text{Total Claims}}$$

Overclaims: The difference between the amount of the EITC claimed by the taxpayer on his or her tax return and the amount the taxpayer should have claimed.

Underpayments: The amount of the EITC disallowed by the IRS in processing that *should have been* allowed.

Claims Protected or Recovered: The amount of EITC overclaims that the IRS prevents from being paid through activities such as math error processing and pre-refund examinations or recovered after post-refund examinations.

Total Claims: The amount of EITC claimed on all tax returns.

Source: Treasury Inspector General for Tax Administration (TIGTA).

Notes: This formula reflects the formula used for FY2013 and subsequent estimates of improper payments.

Figure A-1. Improper Payment Rate Formula.

Do Improper Payments Measure the Cost of EITC Noncompliance to the Government?

The cost of EITC errors to the Treasury equals credit overpayments (overclaims net any overclaims blocked or which were recovered by compliance measures) net of any *underclaims* or *offsetting errors*. An underclaim is the amount of the credit a taxpayer is entitled to claim but neglects to claim, and includes eligible taxpayers who fail to claim the credit entirely as well as those who claim less than they should. An offsetting error is an underclaim that may partially or fully offset an overclaim. For example an offsetting error occurs when a child claimed in error by taxpayer A could have been correctly claimed by taxpayer B, but taxpayer B did not claim that child. Depending on the size of underclaims and offsetting errors, estimated improper payments "may or may not represent a loss to the government."[80]

For example, if tax filers overclaimed $10 billion of the EITC (net of amounts never paid or recovered), but $2 billion of the credit was never claimed by eligible claimants, *the net amount of the credit paid in error* would be $8 billion. When underclaims are large in relation to overclaims, improper payment amount may overstate the cost of EITC errors to the Treasury. When underclaims are relatively small compared to overclaims, improper payment amounts may be accurate approximations of the cost of EITC errors to the Treasury. Currently, there are no publicly available estimates of underclaims and offsetting errors. The IRS does estimate that 21% of eligible EITC claimants do not claim the credit.[81] However, an estimate of the amount of EITC dollars underclaimed by these 21% of eligible recipients is not currently available.

End Notes

[1] Any amount of the credit which is greater than a recipient's tax liability is claimed as a refund on his or her income tax return.

[2] Treasury Inspector General for Tax Administration (TIGTA), The Internal Revenue Service Fiscal Year 2013 Improper Payment Reporting Continues to Not Comply with the Improper Payments Elimination and Recovery Act, March 31, 2014, http://www.treasury.gov/tigta/auditreports/2014reports/201440027fr.pdf.

[3] Improper payments and the improper payment rate must by law be reported annually by a variety of agencies for a variety of programs (P.L. 107-300 as amended by P.L. 111-204 and P.L. 112-248). For more information about the legal requirements of agencies concerning improper payments, see U.S. Government Accountability Office, Improper Payments: Government-Wide Estimates and Reduction Strategies, GAO-14-737T, July 9, 2014, pp. 2-3, http://www.gao.gov/assets/670/664692.pdf.

[4] The Internal Revenue Service, Compliance Estimates for the Earned Income Tax Credit Claimed on 2006-2008 Returns, Publication 5162, Washington, DC, August 2014, http://www.irs.gov/pub/irs-soi/EITCComplianceStudyTY2006-2008.pdf, p. 2.

[5] For more information, see Treasury Inspector General for Tax Administration (TIGTA), The Internal Revenue Service Fiscal Year 2013 Improper Payment Reporting Continues to Not

Comply with the Improper Payments Elimination and Recovery Act, March 31, 2014, http://www.treasury.gov/tigta/auditreports/2014reports/ 201440027fr.pdf.

[6] The source of current data on improper payments in the EITC is the National Research Program (NRP). The NRP uses tax data from a sample that is statistically representative of the taxpayer population. The estimated improper payment rate from the NRP is based on data that is approximately three years old. For example, FY2013 estimates are based on data from 2009 tax returns processed in 2010.

[7] Generally tax provisions are scored as a reduction of revenue. The refundable portion of the EITC however is designated as an outlay, and hence comparable to a spending program. However, noncompliance with other tax laws can result in reduced revenue. The OMB Payment Accuracy does not compare noncompliance in spending programs (improper payments) to noncompliance in tax programs (foregone revenue).

[8] For more information, see the U.S. Government's Payment Accuracy website at https://www.paymentaccuracy.gov/ high-priority-programs.

[9] House Committee on Ways and Means, Subcommittee on Oversight, Written Statement of Nina E. Olson, National Taxpayer Advocate, Hearing on Improper Payments in the Administration of Refundable Credits, http://waysandmeans.house.gov/uploadedfiles/olsen_testimony.pdf, May 25, 2011, p. 9.

[10] The IRS found that in 2006, of the $450 billion in gross tax gap not paid on time, $65 billion will eventually be collected, resulting in a net tax gap of $385 billion. The total tax gap includes tax gaps in the individual, corporate, payroll, and estate tax. For more information, see The Internal Revenue Service, "Tax Gap for Tax Year 2006," press release, January 6, 2012, http://www.irs.gov/pub/newsroom/overview_tax_gap_2006.pdf.

[11] Taxpayer Advocate Service, Fiscal Year 2015 Objectives Report to Congress: Research Initiatives, Washington, DC, p. 158, http://www.taxpayeradvocate.irs.gov/userfiles/file/FY15-Full-Report/Research.pdf.

[12] In addition to the major factors identified in the 2006-2008 EITC Compliance Study that lead to EITC overclaims, the study also identified other minor factors that lead to erroneous claims of the credit. These include errors in applying EITC tie-breaker rules when more than one person can claim a qualifying child, not having a valid Social Security number (SSN), not being a U.S. citizen or resident, not being age 25-64 if claiming the childless EITC, and being the dependent of another taxpayer. In the 2006-2008 EITC Compliance study approximately 700,000 returns annually included one of these errors, resulting in overclaims of between $900 million to $1.4 billion annually. In comparison, the total number of returns with overclaims is estimated at 11.9 million, resulting in between $14.0 billion to $19.3 billion in overclaims annually.

[13] Compliance Estimates for the Earned Income Tax Credit Claimed on 2006-2008 Returns. (2014), p. 6.

[14] Compliance Estimates for the Earned Income Tax Credit Claimed on 2006-2008 Returns. (2014), p. 6.

[15] House Committee on Appropriations, Subcommittee on Financial Services and General Government, Written Statement of Nina E. Olson National Taxpayer Advocate, Hearing on Internal Revenue Service Oversight, 113th Cong., February 26, 2014, http://www.irs.gov/pub/tas/nta_testimony_houseppprops_oversight_022614.pdf, footnote 107, p. 35.

[16] This includes individual income tax returns, corporate tax returns, estate and gift tax returns, employment tax returns and excise tax returns.

[17] Internal Revenue Service Data Book, 2013, p. iii, http://www.irs.gov/pub/irs-soi/13databk.pdf.

[18] Additional tax owed may be a combination of a smaller EITC and a large income tax liability.Internal Revenue Service Data Book, 2013, Table 9a, Examination Coverage, p. 22, http://www.irs.gov/pub/irs-soi/13databk.pdf.

[19] See the Internal Revenue Service website http://www.eitc.irs.gov/Tax-Preparer-Toolkit/dd/consequences.

[20] In cases where a child is the qualifying child of more than one taxpayer and only one of the taxpayers is the child's parent, under the tie-breaker rules for the credit that parent has priority in claiming the child for the credit. However, that does not mean that the parent is required to claim the child for the credit. For more information on the EITC tiebreaker rules, see the IRS's EITC Central webpage at http://www.eitc.irs.gov/EITC-Central/abouteitc/basicqualifications/tiebreaker.

[21] Qualifying children who reside with a service member who is stationed outside the United States while serving on extended active duty with the U.S. Armed Forces are considered to reside in the United States for the purposes of the EITC.

[22] Per IRC §32(c)(3)(A) and its reference to IRC §152(c), a full time student is defined as being at an educational institution for at least five months out of the year in which the credit is claimed.

[23] This excludes qualifying child errors that occur alongside income reporting errors, but does include qualifying child errors that occur in conjunction with other errors, like using an incorrect filing status.

[24] Other EITC qualifying child errors could include errors related to the age test and SSN test for the qualifying child.

[25] Compliance Estimates for the Earned Income Tax Credit Claimed on 2006-2008 Returns. (2014), p. 23.

[26] National Taxpayer Advocate, Fiscal Year 2015 Objectives: Report to Congress, June 30, 2014, p. 124, http://www.taxpayeradvocate.irs.gov/userfiles/file/FY15-Full-Report/The-Earned-Income-Tax-Credit-is-an-EffectiveAnti-Poverty-Tool-That-Requires-a-Non-Traditional-Compliance-Approach-by-the-IRS.pdf.

[27] National Taxpayer Advocate, Fiscal Year 2015 Objectives: Report to Congress, p. 126.

[28] The Economic Growth and Tax Relief Reconciliation Act of 2001 (EGTRRA; P.L. 107-16) "authorizes the IRS beginning in 2004, to use math error authority to deny the earned income credit if the Federal Case Registry of Child Support Orders indicates that the taxpayer is the noncustodial parent of the child with respect to whom the credit is claimed." U.S. Congress, Joint Committee on Taxation, Summary of Provisions Contained in the Conference Agreement for H.R. 1836, the Economic Growth and Tax Relief Reconciliation Act of 2001, committee print, 107th Cong., May 26, 2001, JCX-50-01, p. 6.

[29] V. Joseph Hotz and John Karl Scholz, "Can Administrative Data on Child Support Be Used to Improve the EITC? Evidence from Wisconsin," March 2008, http://www.ssc.wisc.edu/~scholz/Research/EITC_Admin.pdf, p. 2.

[30] In this instance, "summarily deny" means that the IRS identifies the error, adjusts the amount of the credit based on that error and then sends a notice to the EITC claimants indicating the correction has occurred. "Taxpayers then have 60 days to contest the assessment outlined in those notices. Further, if they do not contest the assessment within that time, they lose their right to file an appeal with [the] IRS or the U.S. Tax Court but have the option of filing an amended tax return to be considered by [the] IRS." See U.S. Government Accountability Office, Enhanced Prerefund Compliance Checks Could Yield Significant Benefits, GAO-11-691T, May 25, 2011, p. 4, http://www.gao.gov/assets/130/126283.pdf.

[31] Treasury Inspector General for Tax Administration, The Earned Income Tax Credit Program Has Made Advances; However, Alternatives to Traditional Compliance Methods Are Needed to Stop Billions of Dollars in Erroneous Payments, 2009-40-024, December 31, 2008, p. 9, https://www.treasury.gov/tigta/auditreports/2009reports/ 200940024fr.pdf.

[32] National Taxpayer Advocate, Fiscal Year 2012 Objectives: Report to Congress, June 30, 2011, p. 8, http://www.irs.gov/pub/tas/fy2012_ntaobjectives.pdf.

[33] Janet Holtzblatt, The Challenges to Implementing Health Reform Through the Tax System, The Tax Policy Center, February 2008, p. 9, http://www.taxpolicycenter.org/tpccontent/healthconference_holtzblatt.pdf.

[34] House Committee on Ways and Means, Subcommittee on Oversight, Written Statement of Nina E. Olson National Taxpayer Advocate, Hearing on Improper payments in the Administrations of Refundable Credits, 112th Cong., May 25, 2011, p. 10.

[35] In addition, the Taxpayer Advocate has stressed that when taxpayers' returns are flagged for a potential qualifying child error whereby the taxpayer has not substantiated that the child meets the EITC's residency requirement, these taxpayers also may have difficulty in providing appropriate documentation to prove the child meets the residency test. The Taxpayer Advocate recommended that the IRS require these taxpayers to submit an affidavit instead, which would be easier for taxpayers to obtain. House Committee on Ways and Means, Subcommittee on Oversight, Written Statement of Nina E. Olson National Taxpayer Advocate, Hearing on Improper payments in the Administrations of Refundable Credits, 112th Cong., May 25, 2011, p. 45.

[36] U.S. Government Accountability Office, Enhanced Prerefund Compliance Checks Could Yield Significant Benefits, GAO-11-691T, May 25, 2011, p. 4, http://www.gao.gov/assets/130/126283.pdf.

[37] For additional perspective on income misreporting from previous IRS compliance studies, see Janet Holtzblatt and Janet McCubbin, "Chapter 6: Issues Affecting Low-Income Filers," in The Crisis in Tax Administration, ed. Henry J. Aaron and Joel Slemrod (Washington, DC: Brookings Institution Press, 2004), p. 165.

[38] If earnings are over-reported such that earnings place the tax filer in the "plateau" of the credit, the tax filer will receive a larger credit than he or she is eligible for. If earnings are over reported, such that the tax filer is in the phaseout range of the credit, the tax filer may or may not receive a larger credit.

[39] In 2008, 26.6% of EITC claimants had income that placed them in the phase-in range of the credit, and 21.7% had income that placed them in the plateau region of the credit. See Tax Policy Center, Table T14-0114 at http://taxpolicycenter.org/numbers/displayatab.cfm?Docid=4171&DocTypeID=7.

[40] This excludes income reporting errors that occur alongside qualifying child errors, but includes income reporting errors that occur in conjunction with other errors, like using an incorrect filing status.

[41] This excludes income reporting errors that occur alongside qualifying child errors, but includes income reporting errors that occur in conjunction with other errors, like using an incorrect filing status.

[42] Compliance Estimates for the Earned Income Tax Credit Claimed on 2006-2008 Returns. (2014), p. 20.

[43] Department of the Treasury Internal Revenue Service, IRS Earned Income Tax Credit (EITC) Initiatives: Report on Qualifying Child Residency Certification, Filing Status, and Automated Underrepoter Tests, 2008, p. 23, http://www.irs.gov/pub/irs-utl/final_eitc_initiatives_report_final_121708.pdf.

[44] Government Accountability Office, Tax Refunds: IRS is Exploring Verification Improvements, but Needs to Better Manage Risks, GAO-13-515, June 2013, summary, http://www.gao.gov/assets/660/655020.pdf.

[45] For 2013 levels, see IRS Publication 596, 2013 Earned Income Credit (EIC) Table, http://www.irs.gov/pub/irs-pdf/p596.pdf. The 2014 levels are calculated using the parameters provided in IRS Revenue Procedure 2013-35, http://www.irs.gov/pub/irs-drop/rp-13-35.pdf.

[46] An EITC marriage bonus can occur, for example, when a single parent with no earnings marries a childless individual with low earnings, their EITC as a married couple may be larger than their combined EITCs as singles.

[47] Compliance Estimates for the Earned Income Tax Credit Claimed on 2006-2008 Returns. (2014), p. 20.

[48] Department of the Treasury Internal Revenue Service, IRS Earned Income Tax Credit (EITC) Initiatives: Report on Qualifying Child Residency Certification, Filing Status, and Automated Underrepoter Tests, 2008, p. 20, http://www.irs.gov/pub/irs-utl/final_eitc_initiatives_report_final_121708.pdf.

[49] See Holtzblatt and McCubbin. (2004), p. 170.

[50] Jeffrey B. Liebman, "The EITC Compliance Problem," Poverty Research News, summer 1998, pp. 9-10, http://www.hks.harvard.edu/jeffreyliebman/jcprsurvey.htm.

[51] For more information, see the IRS website, "On EITC Awareness Day, IRS and Partners Alert Low-and Moderate-Income Workers of Significant Tax Benefit" available at http://www.irs.gov/uac/Newsroom/On-EITC-AwarenessDay,-IRS-and-Partners-Alert-Low-and-Moderate-Income-Workers-of-Significant-Tax-Benefit.

[52] Taxpayer Advocate Service, 2013 Annual Report to Congress, Volume 1, p. 61, http://www.taxpayeradvocate.irs.gov/userfiles/file/2013FullReport/REGULATION-OF-RETURN-PREPARERSTaxpayers-and-Tax-Administration-Remain-Vulnerable-to-Incompetent-and-Unscrupulous-Return-Preparers.pdf.

[53] See Holtzblatt and McCubbin. (2004), p. 170.

[54] An unenrolled agent, is by definition, the opposite of an enrolled agent. According to the Internal Revenue Service, "an enrolled agent is a person who has earned the privilege of representing taxpayers before the Internal Revenue Service by either passing a three-part comprehensive IRS test covering individual and business tax returns, or through experience as a former IRS employee. Enrolled agent status is the highest credential the IRS awards. Individuals who obtain this elite status must adhere to ethical standards and complete 72 hours of continuing education courses every three years. Enrolled agents, like attorneys and certified public accountants (CPAs), have unlimited practice rights. This means they are unrestricted as to which taxpayers they can represent, what types of tax matters they can handle, and which IRS offices they can represent clients before." For more information, see http://www.irs.gov/pub/irs-pdf/pcir230.pdf.

[55] Some research suggests that "taxpayers are inclined to seek out preparers who share their values." The National Taxpayer Advocate, 2008 Annual Report to Congress: The Need to Increase Preparer Responsibility, Visibility, and Competence, Volume II, December 31, 2008, p. 80, http://www.irs.gov/pub/tas/08_tas_arc_vol2.pdf.

[56] Compliance Estimates for the Earned Income Tax Credit Claimed on 2006-2008 Returns. (2014), p. 24.

[57] U.S. Government Accountability Office, Paid Tax Return Preparers: In a Limited Study, Preparers Made Significant Errors, GAO-14-467T, April 8, 2014, p. 9, http://www.gao.gov/products/GAO-14-467T. A previous 2006 investigation of paid tax preparers by the

Government Accountability Office (GAO) found that 19 of 19 paid preparers investigated "often prepared returns that were incorrect, with tax consequences that were sometimes significant." In some cases, the errors resulted in unwarranted extra refunds of almost $2,000, while in other cases that taxpayer was actually eligible for more than $1,500 in refund, which the paid preparer did not claim. One common error that GAO found was that the paid tax preparer did not ask where the tax filer's child resided (or ignored the answer), which resulted in an ineligible child being claimed for the EITC in half of the cases they examined. For more information, see U.S. Government Accountability Office, Paid Tax Return Preparers: In a Limited Study Chain Prepares Made Serious Errors, GAO-06- 563T, April 4, 2006, p. 5, http://www.gao.gov/assets/120/113330.pdf.

[58] GAO-14-467T, April 8, 2014, p. 9.

[59] GAO-14-467T, April 8, 2014, p. 12.

[60] See IRS Form 8867, http://www.irs.gov/pub/irs-pdf/f8867.pdf.

[61] Department of the Treasury, General Explanations of the Administration's Fiscal Year 2015 Revenue Proposals, March 2014, p. 238, http://www.treasury.gov/resource-center/tax-policy/Documents/General-ExplanationsFY2015.pdf.

[62] For more information, see http://www.irs.gov/Tax-Professionals/Frequently-Asked-Questions:-Do-I-Need-aPTIN%3F#general.

[63] Four states regulate paid tax preparers, including California, Oregon, Maryland, and New York.

[64] Paid preparers that are already subject to IRS oversight include certified accountants, lawyers, and IRS-enrolled agents who must pass a test and be recertified on a periodic basis by the IRS.

[65] David van den Berg, "EITC Error Rate Grows; Improper Payments Top $13 Billion," Tax Notes, vol. 143 (May 19, 2014), p. 756.

[66] Beginning with the 2011 filing season, the IRS started requiring certain tax preparers to meet testing and continuing education requirements, as well as the requirement that paid preparers obtain PTINs. The IRS launched the registered tax return preparer competency test in November 2011 with a deadline to take the test by December 31, 2013. The continuing education requirements began during the 2012 calendar year. In January 2013, after the new return preparer program was substantially in place, a U.S. district court judge in Loving v. Internal Revenue Service enjoined the IRS from enforcing the testing and continuing education requirements. See http://www.irs.gov/uac/IRS-Proposes-New-Registration,-Testing-and-Continuing-Education-Requirements-for-Tax-Return-Preparers-Not-Already-Subject-to-Oversight and http://www.irs.gov/uac/Newsroom/IRS-Statement-on-Court-Ruling-Related-to-Return-Preparers.

[67] Andrew Velarde and Jaime Arora, "ABA Section of Taxation Meeting: U.S. Won't Take Loving Decision to Supreme Court," Tax Notes, vol. 143 (May 19, 2014), p. 771.

[68] Senate Committee on Finance, Written Testimony of John A. Kiskinen, Commissioner Internal Revenue Service Before the Senate Finance Committee on Regulation of Tax Return Preparers, April 8, 2014, p. 4, http://www.finance.senate.gov/imo/media/ doc/Koskinen%20Testimony.pdf.

[69] See Senate Committee on Finance, Written Testimony of John A. Kiskinen, Commissioner Internal Revenue Service Before the Senate Finance Committee on Regulation of Tax Return Preparers, April 8, 2014, http://www.finance.senate.gov/imo/media/doc/Koskinen%20Testimony.pdf and Department of the Treasury, General Explanations of the Administration's Fiscal Year 2015 Revenue Proposals, March 2014, p. 244,

http://www.treasury.gov/resource-center/tax-policy/Documents/General-Explanations-FY2015.pdf.

[70] For more information, see the http://www.irs.gov/uac/Newsroom/On-EITC-Awareness-Day,-IRS-and-Partners-AlertLow-and-Moderate-Income-Workers-of-Significant-Tax-Benefit.

[71] The IRS Taxpayer Advocate has proposed that the IRS revise its mission statement to encompass social benefits. According to the Taxpayer Advocate, "There are significant differences between benefits agencies and enforcement agencies like the IRS in terms of culture, mindset, and the skill sets and training of their employees. A dual mission statement could serve as an organizing principle toward that end, and would almost make clear that the IRS will require sufficient funding to do both jobs well. Absent adequate funding, the IRS will be forced simultaneously to rob Peter to pay Paul and to rob Paul to pay Peter, and little good will come of that situation." See U.S. Congress, House Committee on Ways and Means, Subcommittee on Oversight, Written Statement of Nina E. Olson, National Taxpayer Advocate, Hearing on Improper Payments in the Administration of Refundable Tax Credits, 112th Cong., May 25, 2011, p. 23, http://www.irs.gov/pub/tas/testimony-written-wm_oversight-improper_payments-5-25-2011.pdf.

[72] Some policymakers have already expressed concern that the improper payment of the EITC is a harbinger of future problems to come with the administration of other refundable tax credits, especially the premium assistance credits enacted as part of the Affordable Care Act (ACA; P.L. 111-148 and P.L. 111-152). For example, see Orrin Hatch, "Think the IRS IS Bad Now? Just Wait." The Wall Street Journal, June 14, 2013, Opinion, http://online.wsj.com/ articles/SB10001424127887323734304578542981761557180.

[73] Improper payments and the improper payment rate must by law be reported annually by a variety of agencies for a variety of programs (P.L. 107-300 as amended by P.L. 111-204 and P.L. 112-248). For more information about the legal requirements of agencies concerning improper payments, see U.S. Government Accountability Office, Improper Payments: Government-Wide Estimates and Reduction Strategies, GAO-14-737T, July 9, 2014, pp. 2-3, http://www.gao.gov/assets/670/664692.pdf.

[74] The Internal Revenue Service, Compliance Estimates for the Earned Income Tax Credit Claimed on 2006-2008 Returns, Publication 5162, Washington, DC, August 2014, http://www.irs.gov/pub/irs-soi/EITCComplianceStudyTY2006-2008.pdf, p. 2.

[75] Internal Revenue Service, Report on Earned Income Tax Credit (EITC) Improper Payments Executive Order 13520: Reducing Improper Payments, Included as an enclosure in the Treasury Inspector General for Tax Administration's (TIGTA) Report 2013-40-084, August 28, 2013, p. 23, http://www.treasury.gov/tigta/auditreports/2013reports/ 201340084fr.pdf.

[76] United States Treasury Department, Agency FY2013 Financial Report, December 16, 2013, p. 206, http://www.treasury.gov/about/budget-performance/annual-performance-plan/Documents/ 2013%20Department%20of%20the%20Treasury%20AFR%20Report%20v2.pdf.

[77] Internal Revenue Service, Report on Earned Income Tax Credit (EITC) Improper Payments Executive Order 13520: Reducing Improper Payments, Included as an enclosure in the Treasury Inspector General for Tax Administration's (TIGTA) Report 2013-40-084, August 28, 2013, p. 23, http://www.treasury.gov/tigta/auditreports/2013reports/ 201340084fr.pdf.

[78] This data used to calculate the improper payment rate will come from 2009 tax data. United States Treasury Department, Agency FY2013 Financial Report, December 16, 2013, p. 206, http://www.treasury.gov/about/budgetperformance/annual-performance-plan/Documents/ 2013%20Department%20of%20the%20Treasury%20AFR%20Report%20v2.pdf.

[79] United States Treasury Department, Agency FY2013 Financial Report, December 16, 2013, p. 206, http://www.treasury.gov/about/budget-performance/annual-performance-plan/Documents/2013%20Department%20of%20the%20Treasury%20AFR%20Report%20v2.pdf.

[80] U.S. Government Accountability Office, Improper Payments: Government-Wide Estimates and Reduction Strategies, GAO-14-737T, July 9, 2014, p. 1, http://www.gao.gov/assets/670/664692.pdf.

[81] See the "EITC Participation Rate by States" on the IRS's EITC Central webpage at http://www.eitc.irs.gov/EITCCentral/Participation-Rate.

In: The Earned Income Tax Credit
Editor: Judith L. Collins

ISBN: 978-1-63485-632-4

Chapter 4

ASSESSMENT OF INTERNAL REVENUE SERVICE COMPLIANCE WITH THE IMPROPER PAYMENT REPORTING REQUIREMENTS IN FISCAL YEAR 2014*

Treasury Inspector General for Tax Administration

ABBREVIATIONS

ACTC	Additional Child Tax Credit
APTC	Advanced Premium Tax Credit
EITC	Earned Income Tax Credit
IPERA	Improper Payments Elimination and Recovery Act
IPERIA	Improper Payments Elimination and Recovery Improvement Act
IPIA	Improper Payments Information Act
IRS	Internal Revenue Service
NRP	National Research Program
OMB	Office of Management and Budget
PTC	Premium Tax Credit
TIGTA	Treasury Inspector General for Tax Administration

* This is an edited, reformatted and augmented version of an audit report, 2015-40-044, issued April 27, 2015.

Highlights

Final Report issued on April 27, 2015 Highlights of Reference Number: 2015-40-044 to the Internal Revenue Service Chief Financial Officer.

Impact on Taxpayers

The Improper Payments Elimination and Recovery Act (IPERA) of 2010 and subsequent legislation strengthened agency reporting requirements and redefined "significant improper payments" in Federal programs. The Office of Management and Budget has declared the Earned Income Tax Credit (EITC) Program a high-risk program that is subject to reporting in the Department of the Treasury (Treasury) Agency Financial Report. The IRS estimates that 27 percent or $17.7 billion in EITC payments were issued improperly in Fiscal Year 2014.

Why TIGTA Did the Audit

This audit was initiated because Treasury Inspector General for Tax Administration (TIGTA) is required to assess the IRS's compliance with the reporting requirements contained in the IPERA;

Executive Order 13520, Reducing Improper Payments and Eliminating Waste in Federal Programs; and the Improper Payment Elimination and Recovery Improvement Act of 2012. The objective of this review was to determine whether the IRS complied with the annual improper payment reporting requirements for Fiscal Year 2014.

What TIGTA Found

The IRS provided all required improper payment information to Treasury for inclusion in the Department of the Treasury Agency Financial Report Fiscal Year 2014 with the exception of reporting an overall EITC improper payment rate below 10 percent. The IRS is unlikely to achieve an improper payment rate below 10 percent without expanded authorities to address identified erroneous claims.

In addition, although the IRS completed risk assessments of the 23 program fund groups identified by Treasury, the risk assessment process still does not provide a valid assessment of improper payments in IRS programs. For example, each year since Fiscal Year 2011, the IRS has continually rated the risk of improper payments associated with the Additional Child Tax Credit (ACTC) as low.

However, our review of the IRS's own enforcement data indicates that the ACTC improper payment rate is similar to that of the EITC. TIGTA estimates that the ACTC improper payment rate for Fiscal Year 2013 is between 25.2 percent and 30.5 percent, with potential ACTC improper payments totaling between $5.9 billion and $7.1 billion.

On March 20, 2014, the Office of Management and Budget issued supplemental improper payment guidance to Treasury clarifying the requirement for annual risk assessments of all refundable tax credits. The Office of Management and Budget guidance clarified that all refundable credits, i.e., the ACTC, are subject to IPERA requirements as they represent an additional outlay of funds by the Government.

TIGTA reported its concern regarding the IRS's incorrect assessment of the risk associated with the ACTC subsequent to the IRS's Fiscal Year 2014 risk assessments. TIGTA will continue to evaluate the reasonableness of the IRS's assessment of the risk of improper refundable tax credit payments when TIGTA reviews the IRS's compliance with the improper payment requirements in Fiscal Year 2015.

What TIGTA Recommended

TIGTA made no recommendations in this report.

April 27, 2015

MEMORANDUM FOR CHIEF FINANCIAL OFFICER

FROM: Michael E. McKenney, Deputy Inspector General for Audit
SUBJECT: Final Audit Report – Assessment of Internal Revenue Service Compliance with the Improper Payment Reporting Requirements in Fiscal Year 2014 (Audit # 201540024)

This report presents the results of our review to determine whether the Internal Revenue Service (IRS) complied with the annual improper payment reporting requirements for Fiscal Year 2014. The Improper Payment Elimination and Recovery Act,[1] Executive Order 13520,[2] and the Improper Payment limitation and Recovery Improvement Act[3] require the Treasury Inspector General for Tax Administration (TIGTA) to review annually the IRS's compliance with these requirements. This audit is included in our Fiscal Year 2015 Annual Audit Plan and addresses the major management challenge of Fraudulent Claims and Improper Payments.

In their response to the draft report, IRS management stated that many of the payments we consider improper are merely misclassifications between the Child Tax Credit and the Additional Child Tax Credit (ACTC). It appears that the IRS is referring to instances in which audit adjustments (such as increases to income or reductions in deductions and credits) cause less of the Child Tax Credit to be refundable.[4] Nonetheless, in these instances, the ACTC was paid in error and these amounts are properly classified as improper payments. We plan to perform further analysis to isolate these instances in our assessment of the IRS's compliance with the improper payment reporting requirements in Fiscal Year 2015.

BACKGROUND

The Office of Management and Budget (OMB) defines an improper payment as any payment that should not have been made, was made in an incorrect amount, or was made to an ineligible recipient. Various ways have been put forth to identify, measure, and reduce Federal improper payments, including laws specifically addressing improper payments, an Executive Order, and guidance by certain oversight agencies such as the OMB. In addition, agency Inspectors General serve a role by evaluating agency information related to improper payments.

The Improper Payments Information Act (IPIA) of 2002[1] requires Federal agencies, including the Internal Revenue Service (IRS), to estimate the amount of improper payments and report to Congress annually on the causes of and the steps taken to reduce improper payments. The IPIA also requires agencies to address whether they have the information systems and other infrastructure needed to reduce improper payments. The annual report must also describe steps the agency has taken to ensure that agency managers are held accountable for reducing improper payments. The following legislation and Executive Order clarified and expanded the IPIA requirements:

- *Executive Order 13520, Reducing Improper Payments and Eliminating Waste in Federal Programs*, signed by the President on November 20, 2009, further increases Federal agencies' accountability for reducing improper payments while continuing to ensure that Federal programs serve and provide access to their intended beneficiaries. It requires Federal agencies to provide their agency Inspector General with detailed information on efforts to identify and reduce the number of improper payments in Federal programs with the highest dollar value of improper payments.
- *Improper Payments Elimination and Recovery Act (IPERA) of 2010*,[2] enacted on July 22, 2010, amended the IPIA by strengthening agency reporting requirements and redefining "significant improper payments." For Fiscal Year[3] 2014 and beyond, significant is defined as gross annual improper payments, i.e., the total amount of overpayments plus underpayments, made in the program during the fiscal year reported that a) exceeded both 1.5 percent of program outlays and $10 million of all program or activity payments or b) exceeded $100 million at any percent of program outlays.
- *Improper Payments Elimination and Recovery Improvement Act (IPERIA) of 2012*,[4] enacted on January 10, 2013, further expanded agency improper payment requirements to foster greater agency accountability. Like Executive Order 13520, the IPERIA requires the OMB Director to identify a list of high-priority Federal programs. For those high-priority programs, the IPERIA requires agencies to develop additional or supplemental measures for tracking progress in reducing improper payments and submit an annual report to the Inspector General of the agency on the steps the agency has taken and plans to take to recover past and prevent future improper payments. The report is also required to be posted on a website accessible to the public.

On October 20, 2014, the OMB issued revisions to Circular A-123 Appendix C, *Requirements for Effective Estimation and Remediation of Improper Payments*. Circular A-123 Appendix C provides agencies and Inspectors General guidance on the implementation of the IPIA as amended by the IPERA, IPERIA, and Executive Order 13520. According to the OMB, the revised Appendix C creates a more unified, comprehensive, and less burdensome improper payment compliance framework. For example, agencies now have the flexibility to combine the various improper payment reporting requirements into one document, the Agency Financial Report. In addition, the agency Inspector General also has the flexibility to conduct one review to assess their respective agency's compliance with the various improper payment requirements.

OMB Guidance on the IRS's Use of Supplemental Measures for Earned Income Tax Credit (EITC)[5] Reduction Targets

According to the Department of the Treasury (Treasury), the complexity of the tax law around the EITC and the significant annual turnover within the participating population makes it difficult to set meaningful improper payment reduction targets. The OMB also recognized the challenges the IRS faces in setting EITC reduction targets. As an alternative, Treasury and the OMB have collaborated on the development of a series of EITC supplemental measures in lieu of EITC reduction targets. The OMB approved the supplemental measures on August 27, 2014, and the measures were published in the *Department of the Treasury Agency Financial Report Fiscal Year 2014* as required. The approved EITC supplemental measures are:

- The Annual Error Rate, which identifies the percentage of total EITC payments that were improper.
- The amount of Revenue Protected, which shows the total value of erroneous payments prevented or recovered through compliance activities.
- The amount of Revenue Protected from Paid Preparer Treatments, which shows dollars erroneously or fraudulently claimed by paid tax preparers but not paid out, or recovered, by Treasury.
- The number of Preparer Due Diligence Penalties Proposed, which reflects the effectiveness of Treasury efforts to ensure that paid tax preparers are submitting accurate, nonfraudulent EITC claims on behalf of taxpayers.

PROCESS TO IDENTIFY IRS PROGRAMS FOR IMPROPER PAYMENT RISK ASSESSMENT

Treasury identifies the programs that the IRS must assess for the risk of improper payments. The IRS used the Improper Payments Elimination and Recovery Risk Assessment Questionnaire for Fiscal Year 2014 (the Questionnaire) and related guidance provided by Treasury to assess the level of risk for each identified program. The Questionnaire computes a risk score for each program based on the IRS's response to the questions contained in the Questionnaire. The risk score determines whether there is a low, medium, or high risk of improper payments in a program. Treasury establishes the level of risk for a program's improper payments based on the risk score ranges and considers programs with a risk score of 0 to 11 as low risk, 12 to 28 as medium risk, and 29 and greater as high risk.

The IRS is required to forward the results and documentation for all risk assessments to the Treasury. Appendix V provides a list of the IRS programs Treasury identified for an improper payment risk assessment for Fiscal Year 2014. For any program identified as having a high risk for improper payments, the IRS must provide the following information to Treasury for inclusion in the Department's annual Agency Financial Report:

- The rate and amount of improper payments.
- The root causes of the improper payments.
- Actions taken to address the root causes.
- Annual improper payment reduction targets.
- A discussion of any limitations to the IRS's ability to reduce improper payments.

The OMB has previously declared the EITC a high-risk program; therefore, no risk assessment is required to be prepared for it. The EITC is currently the only IRS high-risk program and the only one with information included in Treasury's Agency Financial Report. The IRS estimates that 27 percent or $17.7 billion in EITC payments made in Fiscal Year 2014 were paid in error.

In addition, the OMB identifies programs that have a high priority with regard to improper payments. The EITC continues to be the only IRS program the OMB has identified as a high-priority program. As a result, the IRS is responsible for providing the Treasury Inspector General for Tax

Administration (TIGTA) with the information required by the IPERIA and Executive Order 13520.

NATIONAL RESEARCH PROGRAM (NRP) USED TO ESTIMATE EITC IMPROPER PAYMENTS

The IRS uses its NRP as the primary source of data to estimate the annual EITC improper payment rate. The NRP provides the IRS with compliance information that is statistically representative of the taxpayer population. Updated estimates of taxpayer compliance are computed for each tax year.[6] The IRS uses each tax year's NRP results to update the EITC improper payment rate.

Although the NRP process results in a more current estimate of the accuracy of EITC claims than previous methods, the estimated improper payment rate for a given fiscal year is not based on current year data. Because of the time it takes to complete the annual NRP, the IRS's annual estimate of the improper payment rate is based on data that are approximately three years old. For example, EITC improper payment rates for Fiscal Year 2014 are based on information from Tax Year 2010 tax returns that were processed in Calendar Year 2011.[7] Figure 1 shows the improper payment rate formula and figures the IRS used to compute the estimated EITC improper payment rate for Fiscal Year 2014.

Total EITC Improper Payments – Total Claims Protected/Recovered / *Total EITC Claims*
Total EITC Improper Payments – The difference between the amount of the EITC claimed by the taxpayer on his or her tax return and the amount the taxpayer should have claimed. This amount includes EITC overclaims and EITC underpayments. This amount totaled $18.4 billion.[8]
Total Claims Protected/Recovered – The amount of EITC overclaims that the IRS prevents from being paid through prerefund examinations or recovers after being paid through Automated Underreporter document matching and post-refund examinations. This amount totaled $2.2 billion.
Total EITC Claims – The estimated amount of EITC claimed on all tax returns. This amount totaled $59.7 billion.[9]

Source: TIGTA's review of IRS EITC information provided to Treasury for inclusion in the Department of the Treasury Agency Financial Report Fiscal Year 2014.

Figure 1. EITC Improper Payment Rate Formula and Figures Used for Fiscal Year 2014.

PREMIUM TAX CREDIT (PTC)

The Patient Protection and Affordable Care Act[10] (hereafter referred to as the Affordable Care Act) created the Health Insurance Marketplace, also known as the Exchange. The Exchange is where individuals find information about health insurance options, purchase qualified health plans and, if eligible, obtain help paying premiums. The Affordable Care Act also created a new refundable tax credit,[11] the PTC, to assist eligible taxpayers with paying their health insurance premiums. The PTC was not included in the program fund groups selected by Treasury for which the IRS was required to complete the Questionnaire. The funds used to make Advanced PTC (APTC) payments are drawn from the PTC budget fund included in the IRS's budget and subsequently allocated to the Department of Health and Human Services for use in paying the APTC.

This review was performed with information obtained from the Office of the Chief Financial Officer and the Office of Research, Analysis, and Statistics located at the IRS Headquarters in Washington, D.C., and the Wage and Investment Division, Office of Return Integrity and Compliance Services, in Atlanta, Georgia, during the period October 2014 through March 2015. We conducted this performance audit in accordance with generally accepted government auditing standards. Those standards require that we plan and perform the audit to obtain sufficient, appropriate evidence to provide a reasonable basis for our findings and conclusions based on our audit objective. We believe that the evidence obtained provides a reasonable basis for our findings and conclusions based on our audit objective. Detailed information on our audit objective, scope, and methodology is presented in Appendix I. Major contributors to the report are listed in Appendix II.

RESULTS OF REVIEW

Assessment of Internal Revenue Service Fiscal Year 2014 Compliance with Improper Payment Reporting Requirements

The IRS provided all required improper payment information to Treasury for inclusion in the *Department of the Treasury Agency Financial Report Fiscal Year 2014* with the exception of reporting an overall EITC improper payment rate below 10 percent. Figure 2 provides a summary of our evaluation of IRS compliance with the various improper payment requirements.

Improper Payment Requirement	Source of Requirement	Provided by IRS
Conduct a program-specific risk assessment for each program or activity identified by Treasury.	IPERA	Yes
Publish an improper payment estimate for the EITC.	IPERA	Yes
Report an improper payment rate of less than 10 percent for the EITC.	IPERA	No
Provide the methodology for identifying and measuring EITC improper payments.	Executive Order	Yes
Publish annual reduction targets for the EITC and discuss progress toward meeting those targets.[12]	IPERA	Yes
Provide plans and supporting analysis for meeting the reduction targets for EITC improper payments.	Executive Order	Yes
Publish a programmatic corrective action plan for the EITC.	IPERA	Yes

Figure 2. (Continued)

Achieving an Improper Payment Rate Below 10 Percent Is Unlikely Without Expanded Authorities to Address Identified Erroneous Claims

The IPERA requires agencies to report an annual improper payment rate below 10 percent. However, as shown in Figure 3, the IRS has made little improvement in reducing EITC improper payments since it has been required to provide an estimate of these payments to Congress.

In September 2014, we reported that the IRS continues to report significant improper EITC payments each year.[14] Compliance resources are limited, and additional alternatives to traditional compliance methods have not been developed. Consequently, the IRS does not address the majority of potentially erroneous EITC claims. This is despite the fact that the IRS has processes that successfully identify billions of dollars in potentially erroneous EITC payments.

Currently, under the Internal Revenue Code, the IRS can use its math error authority[15] to address erroneous EITC claims by systemically correcting mathematical or clerical errors on EITC claims, such as correcting entries made on the wrong line on the tax return or mathematical errors in computing income or the EITC.

IRS Program	Type of Program	Level of Risk Identified
Qualified School Construction Bonds	Revenue	Low
Refund Collection	Revenue	Low
Refund Collection – Interest	Revenue	Low
Small Business Health Insurance Tax Credit	Revenue	Low

Source: TIGTA's review of IRS EITC information provided to Treasury for inclusion in the Department of the Treasury Agency Financial Report Fiscal Year 2014.

Figure 2. IRS Compliance with Improper Payment Requirements for the EITC Program for Fiscal Year 2014.

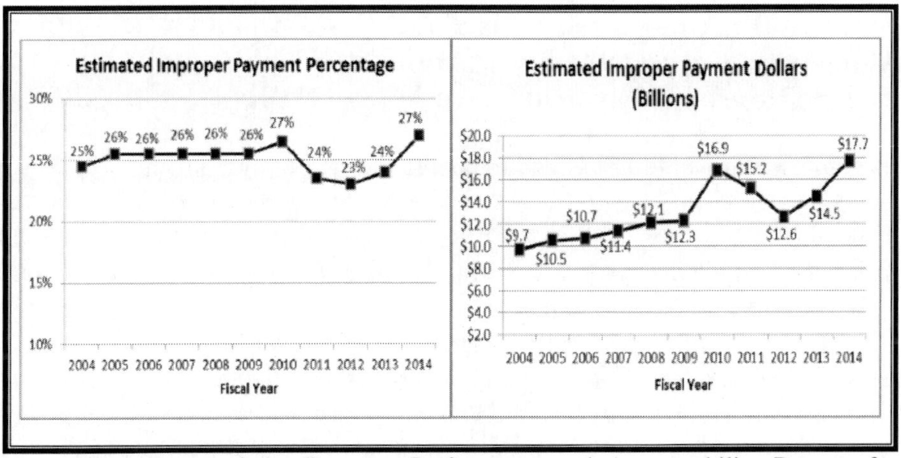

Source: Department of the Treasury Performance and Accountability Reports for Fiscal Years 2004 through 2011, and the Fiscal Years 2012 through 2014 Agency Financial Reports.

Figure 3. Estimated EITC Improper Payments for Fiscal Years 2004 Through 2014.

In addition, the IRS can use math error authority to adjust an EITC claim if a qualifying child's Social Security Number is not valid. However, the majority of potentially erroneous EITC claims the IRS identifies do not contain the types of errors for which it has math error authority. For example, the IRS identified approximately 6.5 million potentially erroneous EITC claims totaling approximately $21.9 billion in Tax Year 2012 for which it does not have math error authority. In Tax Year 2012, the IRS used math error authority to identify and systemically correct only 241,975 (.009 or less than 1 percent) of approximately 27.3 million EITC claims. The 241,975 returns claimed EITCs totaling $299 million.

While the IRS has the authority to audit potentially erroneous EITC claims for which it does not have math error authority, doing so is more costly than the math error process. The IRS estimates that it costs $1.50 to resolve an erroneous EITC claim using math error authority compared to $278 to conduct a prerefund audit. In addition, the number of potentially erroneous EITC claims the IRS can audit is further reduced by its need to allocate its limited resources among the various segments of taxpayer noncompliance to provide a balanced tax enforcement program. As a result, billions of dollars in potentially erroneous EITC claims go unaddressed each year.

National Directory of New Hires Wage and Employment Data Along with Correctable Error Authority Could Significantly Reduce Improper Payments

Legislation would be needed to enable the IRS to systemically disallow a tax claim when information contained in reliable Government data sources does not support the claim. The IRS, in conjunction with the Assistant Secretary of the Treasury for Tax Policy, has put forth a legislative proposal requesting this additional authority (hereafter referred to as correctable error authority). According to the IRS, reliable Government data sources include information obtained from the Social Security Administration, the Department of Health and Human Services, the Federal Bureau of Prisons, and the States' Departments of Corrections. The IRS requested correctable error authority as part of its Fiscal Year 2016 budget submission. However, as of February 2015, the IRS had not been provided any additional authority or tools to expand its ability to prevent the issuance of improper EITC payments.

The IRS is granted the authority to use the National Directory of New Hires to verify EITC claims. However, the IRS does not have the authority to systemically disallow an EITC claim that is not supported by data included in the National Directory of New Hires. Expanded authority to make corrections to tax returns when data obtained from the Department of Health and Human Services indicate the taxpayer's refundable credit claims are not valid would significantly reduce improper payments. For example, the information could be used at the time tax returns are filed to identify those individuals who claim the EITC based on wages that do not appear to be valid. Our review of Tax Year 2012 tax returns identified more than $1.7 billion in potentially erroneous EITCs claimed on tax returns with no third-party Forms W-2, *Wage and Tax Statement*, received by the IRS supporting the wages reported.

Annual Risk Assessments Continue to Underestimate the Risk of Improper Payments in Internal Revenue Service Programs

Our review continues to find that although the IRS completed the risk assessments of the required funds, the risk assessment process does not provide a valid assessment of improper tax refund payments. The EITC remains the only revenue program fund to be considered a high risk for improper payments despite numerous indicators that other refundable tax credits, *i.e.*, the Additional Child Tax Credit (ACTC), also potentially result in significant improper payments.

During the course of this review, we were provided with documentation showing that risk assessments were performed for each of the programs that Treasury required the IRS to assess. Treasury selected 23 IRS program fund groups for review for Fiscal Year 2014 – five administrative program funds and 18 revenue program funds.[16] These funds were selected for assessment based on each fund groups' materiality to the IRS financial statements.

On March 20, 2014, the OMB issued supplemental improper payment guidance to Treasury clarifying the requirement for annual risk assessments of all refundable tax credits. Specifically, the OMB guidance clarified that *all refundable credits* are subject to IPERA requirements as they represent an additional outlay of funds by the Government. However, as we reported in September 2014,[17] risk assessments do not accurately reflect the risk associated with other refundable credit improper payments. For example, Treasury has selected the ACTC as one of the revenue program funds for which the IRS must perform a risk assessment to assess the level of improper payment risk. Treasury selected the ACTC based on its materiality to the IRS's financial statements.

Although the IRS has conducted the annual risk assessment of the ACTC as required by Treasury, each year since Fiscal Year 2011, the IRS has continually rated the risk of improper payments associated with the ACTC as low. The methodology that the IRS uses to conduct the risk assessment continues to provide an inaccurate assessment of the risk of ACTC improper payments. As we reported in our September 2014 report, our review of the IRS's own enforcement data indicates that the ACTC improper payment rate is similar to that of the EITC. We estimate that the ACTC improper payment rate for Fiscal Year 2013 is between 25.2 percent and 30.5 percent, with potential ACTC improper payments totaling between $5.9 billion and $7.1 billion. The OMB defines a program as having significant improper payments when improper payments exceed both 1.5 percent of program outlays and $10 million of all program or activity payments made during the fiscal year reported or exceed $100 million at any percent of program outlays.

In our September 2014 report, we recommended the IRS ensure that the results of the ACTC improper payment risk assessment accurately reflect the high risk associated with ACTC payments and provide a reliable estimate of improper payments and that the assessment should include an evaluation of available NRP and enforcement data when determining the overall risk of improper payments. The IRS disagreed with this recommendation. IRS management stated that the Improper Payment Risk Assessment is completed for the ACTC following the guidance of Treasury and the OMB. The IRS stated that the Questionnaire and scoring methodology reflect operational risks associated with administration of the credit. The IRS further stated that it already considers enforcement data and overall risks associated with administration of the ACTC by its inclusion in the Tax Gap[18] estimate. Notwithstanding the IRS's assertion, the risk associated with ACTC payments is not reflected in the IRS's report on improper payments. This is a concern because the IRS's own enforcement data show that the risk of improper payments associated with the ACTC is similar to that of the EITC – high risk.

We reported our concern regarding the IRS's incorrect assessment of the risk associated with the ACTC after the IRS had conducted its Fiscal Year 2014 risk assessments. We will continue to assess the IRS's compliance on the reporting of improper payments relating to refundable credits when we review the IRS's Fiscal Year 2015 risk assessment rankings. In particular, we will evaluate whether IRS management uses its own enforcement data to accurately reflect the high risk associated with ACTC payments and provide a reliable estimate of improper payments.

The Questionnaire Still Does Not Include Questions to Adequately Address Specific Risks Commonly Associated with Verifying Refundable Credit Claims

In January 2013,[19] we reported that the design of the Questionnaire does not provide an adequate assessment of the risk associated with tax refunds. For example, the Questionnaire contains questions that do not apply to the IRS's revenue program funds. Yet a "yes" or "no" answer to these questions is required. Depending on the response to these questions, the program's risk score can be affected. In addition, questions pertaining to other areas of potential risk in tax administration were not included in the Questionnaire. For example, the Questionnaire does not ask if the IRS has the information it needs to validate a taxpayer's claim for a tax refund at the time the tax return is filed and the tax refund is paid.

In response to our report, the IRS met with Treasury to revise the Questionnaire for revenue funds. Treasury modified the Questionnaire to allow a response of "not applicable" for the questions that do not apply to the IRS's revenue program funds and added a section called Compliance Plan. This section asks if there is an approved compliance plan that identifies the applicable filing, reporting, and payment risks. The section also asks if the compliance plan indicates that pre-processing and/or post-processing filters will be utilized. Treasury also deleted 11 questions from the Questionnaire and added eight new questions. However, the new questions still do not address whether the IRS has the information it needs to validate taxpayer claims at the time the tax return is filed and the refund is paid. The remaining questions are relatively unchanged.

Our review of the revised Questionnaire found that changes are needed to ensure that the Questionnaire provides a valid assessment of the risk of improper tax refund payments. The revised Questionnaire still does not address the risk associated with the IRS not having information it needs to validate a taxpayer's claim for a tax refund at the time the tax return is filed and the tax refund is paid. The IRS continues to inappropriately conclude that tax refund programs for which it conducts a risk assessment have a low risk of improper payments. As a result, the IRS continues to underestimate the risk of improper tax refund payments.

The Structure of the Premium Tax Credit Increases the Complexity of Assessing and Reporting Improper Payments

An agency is usually responsible for complying with the improper payment requirements for payments made from the agency's appropriated funds. Because the funds to make APTC and PTC payments were appropriated to the IRS, it would follow that the IRS will be responsible for assessing the risk of PTC improper payments and complying with the other improper payment requirements. However, the IRS is not solely responsible for administering the PTC. The Department of Health and Human Services Centers for Medicare and Medicaid Services oversees implementation of certain Affordable Care Act provisions related to the Exchanges. The Exchanges have sole responsibility for determining if an individual is eligible to purchase health insurance through the Exchange as well as determining the amount of the APTC they are eligible to receive.

Once the Exchange determines the amount of the APTC an individual is entitled to receive, an individual then elects the actual amount to be sent to his or her insurer on a monthly basis. Individuals can elect to send all, a portion, or none of the APTC to which they are entitled. Once an individual selects his or her insurance coverage and determines the amount of the APTC to be sent to his or her insurer, the insurer submits the information to the Centers for Medicare and Medicaid Services which then sends a request to Treasury's Bureau of the Fiscal Service to issue monthly APTC payments to the individual's insurance provider.

The IRS is responsible for determining the amount of the PTC a taxpayer is entitled to receive. The Affordable Care Act requires all individuals for whom APTC payments were made to an insurer to file a tax return to reconcile the APTC with the actual PTC they are entitled to receive based on the income and family size reported on their tax return.

Because the IRS and the Department of Health and Human Services are responsible for the administration of the PTC, improper PTC payments can result from weaknesses in either agency's programs. As a result, the IRS cannot effectively assess the risk of PTC improper payments, estimate the improper payment rate and dollars, or establish corrective actions to address the causes of and reduce improper PTC payments.

The Department of Health and Human Services began making APTC payments in January 2014 to insurance companies for individuals who purchased insurance covering Calendar Year 2014 through a Health Insurance Exchange. According to IRS management, the OMB established an interagency working group to collaboratively work together to ensure that there is an assessment of risk for improper payments across all payments made from the PTC account. The IRS along with the Department of Health and Human Services Centers for Medicare and Medicaid Services and Treasury are part of the working group. We will evaluate the IRS's improper payment reporting on the PTC in our future annual reviews.

APPENDIX I. DETAILED OBJECTIVE, SCOPE, AND METHODOLOGY

The overall objective of this review was to determine whether the IRS complied with the annual improper payment reporting requirements for Fiscal Year[1] 2014. This review evaluated the IRS's compliance with the reporting requirements contained in the IPERA of 2010;[2] Executive Order 13520, *Reducing Improper Payments and Eliminating Waste in Federal Programs*;[3] and the IPERIA of 2012.[4] The scope of this review included an assessment of the information that the IRS provided for inclusion in the *Department of the Treasury (Treasury) Agency Financial Report Fiscal Year 2014* and a review of the IRS's progress on previous recommendations. To accomplish our objective, we:

I. Determined if conditions identified in prior TIGTA audits still exist. We reviewed Treasury's Joint Audit Management Enterprise System reports, discussed the IRS's corrective actions with management, and determined if the previous recommendations and goals had been implemented.
   A. Determined the methodology used to develop supplemental measures to be used in lieu of EITC improper payment reduction targets.
   B. Determined if improvements have been made to the IPERA risk assessment process.

II. Reviewed the Department of the Treasury Agency Financial Report Fiscal Year 2014 published on November 17, 2014, to determine if the IRS was in compliance with the improper payment reporting requirements for Fiscal Year 2014. We compared the information contained in the Agency Financial Report to the improper payment reporting requirements outlined in the OMB Circular A-123, Management's Responsibility for Internal Control, guidance on improper payment reporting.
   A. Determined if the IRS was in compliance with IPERA reporting elements.
   B. Determined if the IRS was in compliance with IPERIA reporting elements.
   C. Determined if the IRS was in compliance with Executive Order 13520 reporting elements.

D. Reviewed the information that the IRS provided to Treasury for posting to the paymentaccuracy.gov website.

E. Evaluated the accuracy and reasonableness of the IRS's estimate of the EITC improper payment rate. We also evaluated the IRS computations of the overall EITC improper payment rate and associated dollar projections to verify they were accurate.

III. Determined how PTC improper payments are to be accounted for under improper payment legislation. We obtained support for decisions made by the OMB with regard to how the risk of PTC improper payments should to be evaluated.

Internal Controls Methodology

Internal controls relate to management's plans, methods, and procedures used to meet their mission, goals, and objectives. Internal controls include the processes and procedures for planning, organizing, directing, and controlling program operations. They include the systems for measuring, reporting, and monitoring program performance. We determined that the following internal controls were relevant to our audit objective: controls in place to ensure that the IRS met the annual improper payment reporting requirements established in the IPERA, Executive Order 13520, and the IPERIA. We tested these controls by reviewing and analyzing relevant documents, data, and calculations related to the preparation of EITC improper payment estimate information.

Appendix II. Major Contributors to This Report

Russell P. Martin, Acting Assistant Inspector General for Audit (Returns Processing and
Account Services)
Deann L. Baiza, Director
Sharla J. Robinson, Audit Manager
Roy E. Thompson, Audit Manager
Jane G. Lee, Lead Auditor
W. George Burleigh, Senior Auditor
Jennie G. Choo, Senior Auditor
Sandra L. Hinton, Senior Auditor

APPENDIX III. REPORT DISTRIBUTION LIST

Commissioner C
Office of the Commissioner – Attn: Chief of Staff C
Deputy Commissioner for Operations Support OS
Deputy Commissioner for Services and Enforcement SE
Commissioner, Wage and Investment Division SE:W
Chief Counsel CC
Director, Office of Research, Analysis, and Statistics RAS
Director, Office of Legislative Affairs CL:LA
Director, Office of Program Evaluation and Risk Analysis RAS:O
Director, Office of Research RAS:R
Director, Return Integrity and Compliance Services, Wage and Investment Division SE:W:RICS
National Taxpayer Advocate TA
Office of Internal Control OS:CFO:CPIC:IC
Audit Liaisons:
Chief Financial Officer CFO
Office of Research, Analysis, and Statistics RAS
Chief, Program Evaluation and Improvement, Wage and Investment Division SE:W:S:PEI

APPENDIX IV. TREASURY INSPECTOR GENERAL FOR TAX ADMINISTRATION AUDIT REPORTS ON IMPROPER PAYMENTS

TIGTA, Ref. No. 2015-40-009, The Internal Revenue Service Is Working Toward Compliance With Executive Order 13520 Reporting Requirements (Dec. 2014).

TIGTA, Ref. No. 2014-40-093, Existing Compliance Processes Will Not Reduce the Billions of Dollars in Improper Earned Income Tax Credit and Additional Child Tax Credit Payments (Sept. 2014).

TIGTA, Ref. No. 2014-40-027, The Internal Revenue Service Fiscal Year 2013 Improper Payment Reporting Continues to Not Comply With the Improper Payments Elimination and Recovery Act (Mar. 2014).

TIGTA, Ref. No. 2013-40-084, The Internal Revenue Service Is Not in Compliance With Executive Order 13520 to Reduce Improper Payments (Aug. 2013).

TIGTA, Ref. No. 2013-40-024, The Internal Revenue Service Was Not in Compliance With All Requirements of the Improper Payments Elimination and Recovery Act for Fiscal Year 2012 (Feb. 2013).

TIGTA, Ref. No. 2012-40-028, The Internal Revenue Service Is Not in Compliance With All Improper Payments Elimination and Recovery Act Requirements (Mar. 2012).

TIGTA, Ref. No. 2011-40-023, Reduction Targets and Strategies Have Not Been Established to Reduce the Billions of Dollars in Improper Earned Income Tax Credit Payments Each Year (Feb. 2011).

APPENDIX V. INTERNAL REVENUE SERVICE PROGRAMS IDENTIFIED FOR IMPROPER PAYMENT RISK ASSESSMENTS

The following IRS programs were identified by the Department of the Treasury for improper payment risk assessments for Fiscal Year 2014.

IRS Program	Type of Program	Level of Risk Identified
Affordable Health Care Program	Administrative	Low
Business Systems Modernization	Administrative	Low
Information Systems	Administrative	Low
Tax Law Enforcement	Administrative	Low
Taxpayer Services	Administrative	Low
Adoption Credit	Revenue	Low
Alternative Minimum Tax Credit Refunds	Revenue	Low
American Opportunity Credit	Revenue	Low
Build America Bonds	Revenue	Low
Child (Tax) Credit Payments	Revenue	Low
Consolidated Omnibus Budget Reconciliation Act Credit	Revenue	Low
Corporation Tax Credit Refunds	Revenue	Low
EITC Disbursements[1]	Revenue	High
Health Care Credit Payments	Revenue	Low
Home Buyers Credit Refunds	Revenue	Low
Informant Reimbursement	Revenue	Low
New Clean Renewable Energy Bonds	Revenue	Low
Qualified Energy Conservation Bond	Revenue	Low

IRS Program	Type of Program	Level of Risk Identified
Qualified Zone Academy Bonds	Revenue	Low
Qualified School Construction Bonds	Revenue	Low
Refund Collection	Revenue	Low
Refund Collection – Interest	Revenue	Low
Small Business Health Insurance Tax Credit	Revenue	Low

Source: IRS Office of the Chief Financial Officer.

End Notes for Memorandum

[1] Pub. L. No. 111-204, 124 Stat. 2224.

[2] Executive Order 13520, Reducing Improper Payments and Eliminating Waste in Federal Programs (November 20, 2009).

[3] Pub. L. No. 112-248, 126 Stat. 2390.

[4] The ACTC is the refundable portion of the Child Tax Credit.

End Notes

[1] Pub. L. No. 107-300, 116 Stat. 2350.

[2] Pub. L. No. 111-204, 124 Stat. 2224.

[3] Any yearly accounting period, regardless of its relationship to a calendar year. The Federal Government's fiscal year begins on October 1 and ends on September 30.

[4] Pub. L. No. 112-248, 126 Stat. 2390.

[5] Congress originally approved the EITC legislation in 1975 in part to offset the burden of Social Security taxes and to provide an incentive to work. The EITC is a refundable tax credit that offsets income tax owed by low-income taxpayers. A refundable tax credit is one that exceeds the amount of taxes due; it generally provides a lump-sum payment in the form of a refund to those who qualify.

[6] A 12-month accounting period for keeping records on income and expenses used as the basis for calculating the annual taxes due. For most individual taxpayers, the tax year is synonymous with the calendar year.

[7] Tax Year 2010 was the most current NRP data available at the time the IRS computed the estimated Fiscal Year 2014 improper payment rate.

[8] According to IRS management, $18.6 billion reported in the Department of the Treasury Agency Financial Report Fiscal Year 2014 was the preliminary amount.

[9] The IRS uses an estimate for current year EITC claims because it does not know the actual amount at the time it is required to submit improper payment estimates to Treasury for inclusion in the Agency Financial Report. The estimate of EITC claims is based on a budget projection prepared by Treasury's Office of Tax Analysis. The IRS's most recent estimate is $65.2 billion.

[10] Pub. L. No. 111-148, 124 Stat. 119 (2010) (codified as amended in scattered sections of the U.S. Code), as amended by the Health Care and Education Reconciliation Act of 2010, Pub. No. 111-152, 124 Stat.1029.

[11] Refundable tax credits can be used to reduce a taxpayer's tax liability to zero. Any excess of the credit beyond the tax liability can be refunded to the taxpayers.

[12] Supplemental measures were established in lieu of reduction targets.

[13] The recently issued OMB guidance revised improper payment requirements effective for Fiscal Year 2014 forward which raised the dollar threshold for which agencies are required to report quarterly high-dollar improper payments from $5,000 per individual to $25,000 per individual. Because the maximum EITC an individual can receive is well below the revised $25,000 threshold, the IRS would not be required to report any quarterly high-dollar payments for Fiscal Year 2014 forward.

[14] TIGTA, Ref. No. 2014-40-093, Existing Compliance Processes Will Not Reduce the Billions of Dollars in Improper Earned Income Tax Credit and Additional Child Tax Credit Payments (Sept. 2014).

[15] The IRS is granted math error authority in 26 U.S.C. § 6213(b). It can be used for certain purposes specified by Congress in 26 U.S.C. § 6213(g)(2) including correcting calculation errors and checking for other obvious noncompliance, such as claims above income and credit limits. If it is not specified in statute, the IRS cannot pursue assessment and collection activities without issuing a statutory notice of deficiency.

[16] See Appendix V. Note: The EITC Program has been declared a high-risk program for improper payments by the OMB; therefore, no formal risk assessment is required for it.

[17] TIGTA, Ref. No. 2014-40-093, Existing Compliance Processes Will Not Reduce the Billions of Dollars in Improper Earned Income Tax Credit and Additional Child Tax Credit Payments (Sept. 2014).

[18] The Tax Gap is the estimated difference between the amount of tax that taxpayers should pay and the amount that is paid voluntarily and on time.

[19] TIGTA, Ref. No. 2013-40-015, Improper Payments Elimination and Recovery Act Risk Assessments of Revenue Programs Are Unreliable (Jan. 2013).

End Notes for Appendix I

[1] Any yearly accounting period, regardless of its relationship to a calendar year. The Federal Government's fiscal year begins on October 1 and ends on September 30.

[2] Pub. L. No. 111-204, 124 Stat. 2224.

[3] Executive Order 13520, Reducing Improper Payments and Eliminating Waste in Federal Programs (November 20, 2009).

[4] Pub. L. No. 112-248, 126 Stat. 2390.

End Note for Appendix V

[1] The EITC Program has been declared a high-risk program for improper payments by the OMB; therefore, no formal risk assessment is required for it.

INDEX

D

E

F

G

N

O

P

R

S